DiDA

DIPLOMA IN DIGITAL APPLICATIONS

D201: Using ICT

P.M. Heathcote & R.S.U. Heathcote

PAYNE-GALLWAY
PUBLISHERS LTD

www.payne-gallway.co.uk

Acknowledgements

Published by Payne-Gallway Publishers Limited
Payne-Gallway is an imprint of Harcourt
Education Ltd., Halley Court, Jordan Hill,
Oxford, OX2 8EJ

Copyright © P.M. Heathcote and
R.S.U. Heathcote 2005

First published 2005

10 09 08 07 06 05
10 9 8 7 6 5 4 3 2 1

British Library Cataloguing in Publication Data
is available from the British Library on request

ISBN 1 904467 65 2

Copyright notice

Cover picture © Richard Chasemore 2005

Design and Typesetting by Direction Marketing
and Communications Ltd

Printed in Malta by Gutenberg Press Ltd

Ordering Information

You can order from:

Payne-Gallway,
FREEPOST (OF1771),
PO Box 381, Oxford OX2 8BR

Tel: 01865 888070
Fax: 01865 314029
E-mail: orders@payne-gallway.co.uk
Web: www.payne-gallway.co.uk

We would like to thank Rosemary Richards for permission
to use material from *Intermediate GNVQ Information and
Communication Technology*, and *Pass ECDL Module 2*,
both published by Payne-Gallway.

**We are grateful to the following organisations for
permission to use copyright material:**

http://gordonye/yegifs/panda1_sm Gordon Ye (Panda)

http://imaginationfilm.tv/gallery.htm ImagiNation
Productions (Poisonous dart frog)

www.kodiak.org/images/bearb2 US Department of Fish
and Wildlife (Brown bear)

www.oceanexplorer.noaa.gov/explorations/02hawaii/
background/monk_seals/monk_seals.html Chad
Yoshinaga (Monk seal)

www.southafrica.net Strategic Research Unit, South
African Tourism (Rhino and baby)

Patrick M. Rose, Save the Manatee Club
www.education@savethemanatee.org (Manatee)

WWF-UK Image No: 37167 Indian Tiger, Thailand ©
WWF-Canon / Martin Harvey

Google, screenshots p. 218 copyright © Google

The Guardian, screenshot p. 213 Copyright Guardian
Newspapers Limited 2004

Microsoft product screen shots reprinted with permission
from Microsoft Corporation.

Suffolk County Library

WWF

www.gbwebdesign.com/jaguar.html

Promotion posters p.147 © www.superglider.com

Every effort has been made to contact copyright owners
of material published in this book. We would be glad
to hear from unacknowledged sources at the earliest
opportunity.

Section One
PROJECT WORK

The project

For this unit you will be given a scenario by Edexcel. You will need to do some research on the topic set, and produce various documents as specified in the brief. You will then put all these documents into an eportfolio, which will be assessed by the Exam Board; in Chapter 17 you will learn more about the eportfolio and how to put it together. You will be expected to spend a minimum of 30 hours on the project.

Some of the work can be done in a group, but it is very important that your own input is clearly identified. For example, the task of collecting survey results and inputting them into a spreadsheet might be shared between members of a group. Each member, however, should do their own individual analysis of the results.

In order to practise the skills required for the set project, you will work through a sample project of a similar nature in this book. You can view the finished eportfolio, similar to the one you will produce, online at

www.payne-gallway.co.uk/didaD201/eportfolio.

The scenario

The Global Environment Association (GEA) is a charity dedicated to preserving the natural environment and plant and animal species in all parts of the world.

Note:

This charity is not a real one, though many charities, like the WWF, exist to do similar work.

The GEA has been invented for this assignment. Any similarity to real organisations, past or present, is purely coincidental.

There are many threats to wildlife which the GEA are working to reduce. These include:

- climate change;
- destruction of marine habitat, and over-fishing;
- deforestation;
- illegal trade in animal products, such as tiger bones, ivory, and rhino horn.

What can you do about it?

The GEA has recruited volunteers in schools and colleges to help increase awareness of the issues and raise funds to help with their work. You have volunteered to be the representative for your school.

You will use ICT for much of your work – for example:

- to find out how much people know about environmental issues and endangered species;
- to find out whether people care about species becoming extinct and are prepared to take action;
- to inform and persuade others of the value of the GEA's work.

You will be creating posters, leaflets, surveys and presentations. It is vital when creating each of these that you remember who you are aiming it at. If you get it right, you will find that the publications you create will actually work in educating and persuading others.

Planning your project

For your eportfolio you must produce a detailed plan of how you will complete all the required tasks within the time allowed.

Before you start the plan:

- read through the project brief;
- make a list of everything you have to do;
- decide how long you think each element is going to take;
- decide on the order in which the tasks need to be done;
- decide at what points you need to get feedback and to evaluate your work.

At regular intervals you must make sure that you are on schedule; if you are not, you must reschedule the remaining tasks into the time you have left to complete the project. **Keep a record of changes made to your schedule.**

The project brief

The Edexcel Summative Project Brief (SPB) is specified on their website and is spread over a number of pages. When the time comes for you to start the SPB, you will have to explore the website and make a list of what you have to do, similar to the list below.

For this sample project, the tasks are given and each one will be explained in more detail in later chapters in the book.

Here are the tasks which you must complete:

1   Produce a plan listing individual tasks and estimated completion dates.

2   Create an organised directory structure for your project files.

3   Gather information for a leaflet about endangered species and what can be done to save them.

4   Design and produce the leaflet.

5   Produce a questionnaire for a survey on environmental issues.

6   Design a spreadsheet to record the results.

7   Use formulae to analyse the results, and produce charts.

8   Present the results of the survey, to help GEA target their marketing more effectively.

9   Create an interactive information point for display in the school to raise awareness of GEA's work and to advertise a fundraising concert.

10   Create a database of donors and import existing data.

11   Design the data entry form for inputting new donors.

12   Extract information from the database using queries.

13   Design a report showing the names of donors and other details.

14   Design a poster advertising the concert.

15   Design a flyer advertising the concert.

16   Write a letter to the band, thanking them for playing at the concert.

17   Get feedback and evaluate the project.

18   Create the eportfolio.

Creating a project plan

Projects are unlikely to succeed unless they are properly planned. However, before you can start to plan, you have to be absolutely clear about the purpose of the project and what you are required to produce.

You should read the entire project brief first. There are a number of key questions you need to ask, including:

- what do I have to produce?
- what is it for?
- who is the intended audience?
- when do I have to have it finished?
- what resources can I use?
- how will the success of the project be judged?
- who will review my work and when?

There are several ways of creating a plan and you can choose a way that you like the best. Two methods you could use are:

1   a table;

2   a calendar.

Example 1: A table

▶ Open a new Word document.

▶ From the main menu, select **Table**, **Insert**, **Table**.

▶ Select **4** columns by **20** rows.

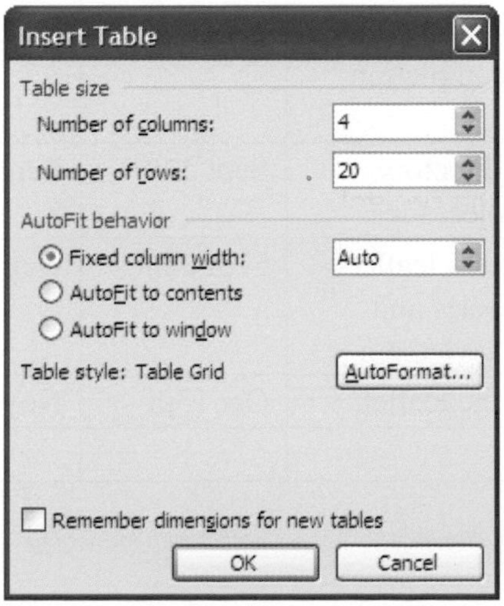

Figure 1.1: Creating a table

The table will appear.

▶ Fill in the table with your plan. The first few lines are shown below.

Task Number	Description	Start Date	End Date
1	Produce a plan listing individual tasks and estimated completion dates.	Sept 20th	Sept 26th
2	Create an organised directory structure for my project files.	Sept 27th	Sept 27th
3	Gather information for a leaflet about endangered species and what can be done to save them.	Sept 28th	Oct 12th
4	Design and produce the leaflet.	Oct 13th	Nov 9th
5	Etc.		

Figure 1.2: A tabular plan

▶ You need another column for notes. Insert it by clicking in the right-hand column, then selecting **Table**, **Insert**, **Columns to the Right** from the main menu.

▶ Adjust the column widths by dragging the column boundaries to the left or right.

▶ Make the column headings **Bold**. You can change the font and centre some of the headings if you wish.

Task Number	Description	Start Date	End Date	Notes
1	Produce a plan listing individual tasks and estimated completion dates.	Sept 20th	Sept 26th	
2	Create an organised directory structure for your project files.	Sept 27th	Sept 27th	
3	Gather information for a leaflet about endangered species and what can be done to save them.	Sept 28th	Oct 12th	
4	Design and produce the leaflet.	Oct 13th	Nov 9th	
5	Etc.			

Figure 1.3: A tabular plan with formatting

Save the plan as **GEA Project Plan.doc** in a suitable folder. In the next chapter you will create a folder structure for the entire project and you can move it into a different folder then.

Example 2: A calendar

An alternative way to plan your project is to assign each of the tasks to a date in a calendar.

You need to produce a calendar in Word or Publisher, like in Figure 1.4, rather than writing tasks into a pre-printed calendar by hand. This is because you will need to submit an electronic version to be assessed in your eportfolio. You will also find that, as time goes on, you will inevitably need to make adjustments to your schedule. Don't overwrite the original schedule – save each new version as **GEA Project Plan v2.doc**, **GEA Project Plan v3.doc** etc.

 Create a table in Word by clicking on **Table**, **Insert**, **Table** on the main menu.

 Select a table **5** columns wide by **10** rows. You can always add more rows as you type in your tasks.

 Enter the headings **Start Date**, **Duration**, **Task Number and Description** and **Notes** into the top right cells and make them **Bold**.

 In the second column, enter the dates of the start of each week, one per row.

 In the third column, enter the number of weeks you expect to spend on the task.

 Now position the cursor over each of the column boundaries. When it changes into a two-way arrow, drag it to resize the columns.

 Highlight the two cells to the left of the first month's dates and select **Table**, **Merge Cells**.

	Start Date	**Duration**	**Task Number and Description**	**Notes**
	20th			
	27th			
	4th			
	11th			
	18th			
	25th			
	2nd			
	9th			

Figure 1.4

 Right-click in the new merged cell and select **Text Direction**. Choose the upward **Orientation**. Click **OK**.

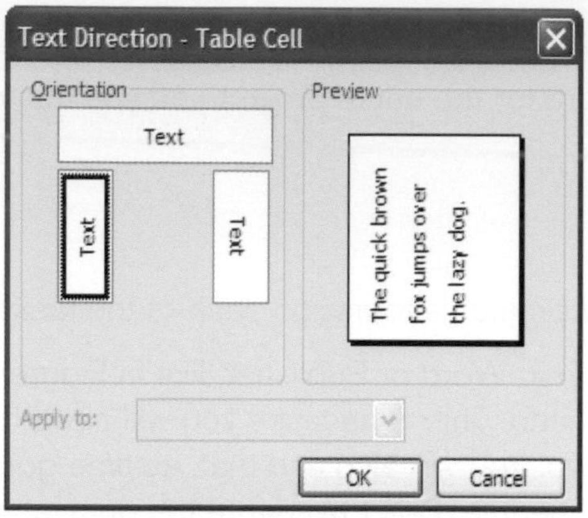

Figure 1.5: Changing text direction

- ▶ Type **Sept** into the cell and make it **Bold**.

- ▶ Right-click in the cell again and select **Cell Alignment**. Choose the centre option.

- ▶ Now select **Borders and Shading** from the pop-up menu and shade in the cell.

- ▶ Repeat the steps for the months of Oct and Nov.

- ▶ Type in the first task, to produce a plan for 20th September.

- ▶ Click the **Numbering** button on the toolbar to number the task.

- ▶ Fill in the calendar with the rest of the project tasks. Use **Table**, **Merge Cells** to merge weeks together for longer tasks. See Figure 1.6.

	Start Date	Time	Task Number and Description	Notes
Sept	20th	1 week	1. Produce a plan listing individual tasks and estimated completion dates.	
	27th	1 week	2. Create an organised directory structure for your project files.	
Oct	4th	1 week	3. Gather information for a leaflet about endangered species and what can be done to save them.	
	11th	4 weeks	4. Design and produce the leaflet.	
	18th			
	25th			
Nov	2nd			
	9th		5. Etc.	

Figure 1.6: A calendar of tasks

⊚ Save this plan as **GEA Project Plan (calendar).doc**.

⊚ Decide which type of plan you like best and complete one of them, putting in your own dates and activities.

Good marks... ✓

You will get good marks if you:

- read the SPB carefully and make a list of everything you need to do;
- use a table, calendar or chart for your plan that includes
    - task numbers
    - a description of each task
    - the date you will start each task
    - the date you will finish each task, and/or time allowed for each task
    - space for any notes relevant to each task
    - a sensible order for the tasks
    - extra time built in to your plan for emergencies or any problems;
- agree your plan with your teacher;
- meet your deadlines by sticking to your plan;
- keep a record of the changes you make to your plan.

Bad marks... ✗

You will lose marks if you:

- set yourself an unrealistic timetable;
- produce your plan but don't use it;
- produce your plan *after* you have completed your project;
- produce a plan that is the same as everyone else's.

Once you have had a good look at the Project Brief, made a list of all the tasks and made a plan of how you are going to get them all done, you can get started!

Task 1 (Produce a plan) is already done.

Task 2 (Create an organised directory structure for your project files) needs to be tackled now.

In this chapter we will look at one possible way that you might choose to organise your project work. Then you can create a directory structure on your computer to hold all your files.

Grouping the tasks

Look at the list of 18 tasks on page 4. Which of these tasks will result in an actual document or file being produced? What software will you use for each task?

You could start by making a table.

Task	Software	Output
2	Windows Explorer	Directory Structure
3–4	Publisher	Leaflet
5	Word	Questionnaire
6–7	Excel	Spreadsheet
8	PowerPoint	Presentation
9	PowerPoint	Presentation
10–13	Access	Database
14	Publisher	Poster
15	Publisher	Flyer
16	Word	Letter
17	Word	Report
18	Word?	Eportfolio

Now you can think about grouping the tasks in some logical way. For example, there are four tasks which could be done using Publisher (though you may decide to use different software). One way of grouping the tasks would be to put all the tasks to be done in a particular software package in the same folder, perhaps divided into sub-folders. That would be quite logical, and if you change your mind about the software to be used, you can always amend your folder structure.

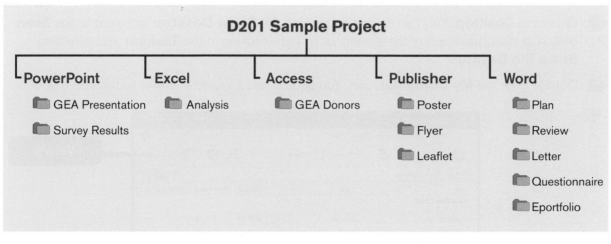

Figure 2.1

Alternatively, you could group the tasks according to the subject matter they deal with. For example, there are four or five tasks (9,14–17) which are all to do with a fund-raising concert. There are three tasks (5, 6 and 8) which are about a survey – producing a questionnaire, entering, analysing and presenting results.

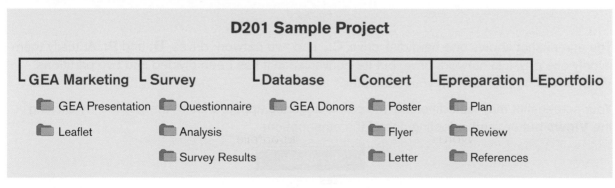

Figure 2.2

When you come to do your own project, following the **Summative Project Brief** (SPB) set by Edexcel, you will have to make your own decisions about how to organise your files into directories.

In this chapter we will create a directory structure which corresponds to Figure 2.2.

Disk drives on your computer

You probably have several disk drives on your computer. Windows assigns a letter to each of them. The floppy drive is usually **A:**, the hard drive **C:**, the zip drive (if you have one) is probably **D:**, the CD drive **E:**, and so on. On a network, the hard drive is usually divided (or 'partitioned') into several 'logical drives' called, for example, **F:, G:, H:** etc.

You can see what drives your computer has, and how much free space there is on each disk.

⊙ Go to the **Desktop**. You can do this by clicking the **Show Desktop** icon next to the **Start** button at the bottom left of the screen, or by right-clicking in the **Taskbar** and selecting **Show the Desktop**.

⊙ Double-click the **My Computer** icon. You should see a window similar to the one below:

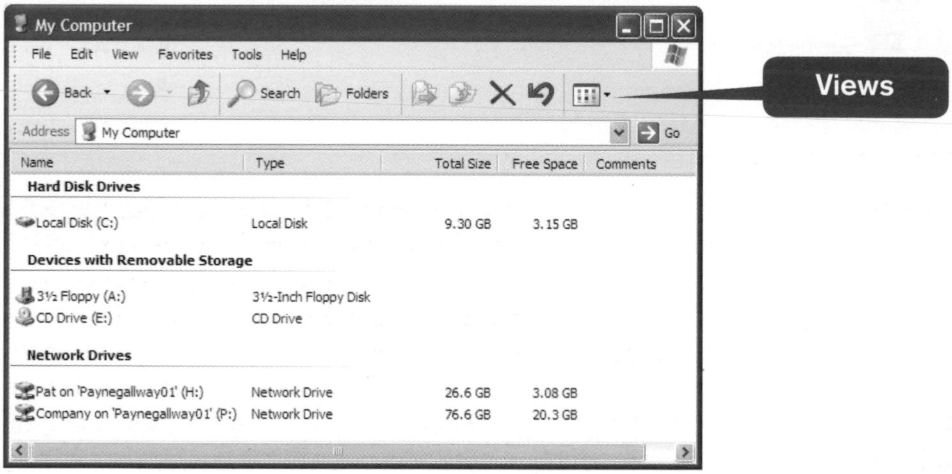

Figure 2.3

The screenshot shows one hard disk drive, **C:,** and two network drives, **H:** and **P:**. Actually there is only one physical network drive, but for convenience it has been divided into two partitions. What drives do you have on your computer?

Views

Your screenshot may look different. You can change the appearance of the window by clicking the **Views** button, and selecting one of the other options.

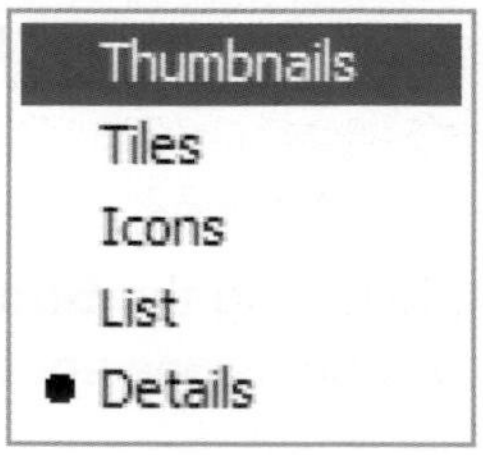

Figure 2.4

Directories/folders

All the documents you create on your PC are referred to as files. These files have to be given names (you can use up to 255 characters) and it is a good idea to use meaningful filenames so that you can easily find a particular file later on.

As you use your computer more and more you will have lots of files stored on your hard drive (**C:**). You will need to keep your work organised so that you can go to it quickly.

Files are organised by saving them into folders, which are also given names. These folders can contain sub-folders. One very important folder, which is set up automatically for you, is **My Documents**. This is where **Windows** expects you to create your own sub-folders to store your work.

My Documents

Tip:

You will see the **My Documents** icon on the desktop.

We are going to set up a folder structure within **My Documents** to match Figure 2.2. Each of these folders will probably contain several files. For example, in the **GEA Presentation** folder (itself a sub-folder of **GEA Marketing**) you will probably keep all the graphics for the presentation, one or more rough drafts and the final presentation, which could be named, for example, **GEA Interactive.ppt**.

Important Note:

You need to keep some early versions of each task to put in the eportfolio. Marks are given for checking, modification and refinement of work, taking account of feedback from others.

The location of a file is specified by its path. For example, looking at Figure 2.2, the path to the presentation **GEA Interactive.ppt** would be as follows:

C:\My Documents\D201 Sample Project\GEA Marketing\GEA Presentation\GEA Interactive.ppt.

▶ Double-click the **C:** drive icon.

You will now see a window displaying the folders on the **C:** drive. (Your window will have different folders.)

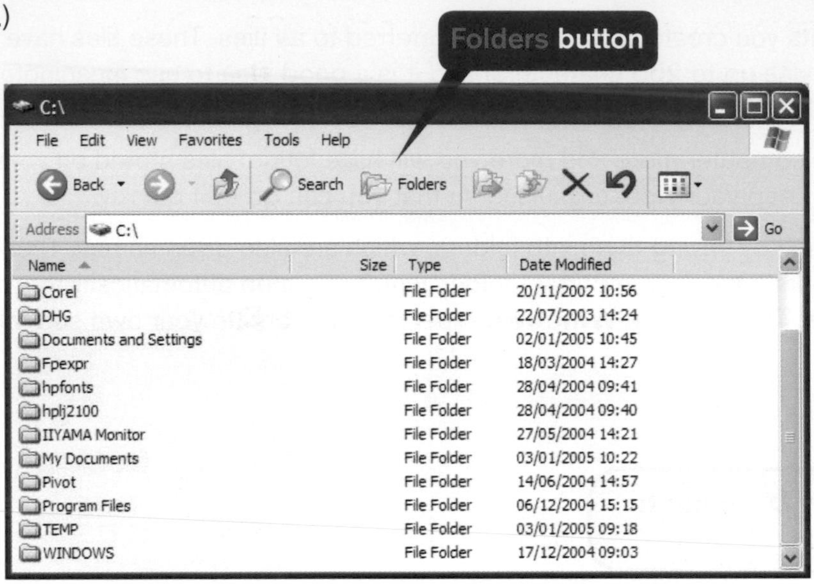

Figure 2.5

Click the **Folders** button if it is not already selected. This shows you a more detailed view.

Figure 2.6

Tip:

The view shown above is the **Details** view. Click the **Views** button to change to this view if your screen looks different.

Creating a new folder

We will set up the folders and subfolders shown in Figure 2.2.

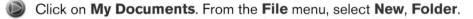 Click on **My Documents**. From the **File** menu, select **New, Folder**.

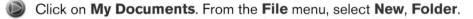 Type **D201 Sample Project** as the name and press **Enter**.

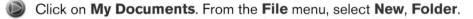 Click the **D201 Sample Project** folder in the tree and create the sub-folder **GEA Marketing**.

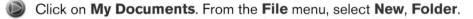 Click the **D201 Sample Project** folder again.

Create the other five folders **Survey**, **Database**, **Concert, Epreparation** and **Eportfolio** in the same way.

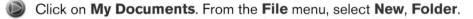 Now create the sub-folders in each of these folders.

Navigating to a file or folder

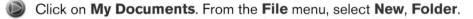 In the left-hand pane, click **GEA Marketing**. Now you should see all the sub-folders you created within that folder.

Figure 2.7

Notice that you can now see the hierarchy of folders and files: when you clicked **My Documents**, the little **+** sign beside it in the left-hand window changed to a **−** sign. The **+** sign indicates that there are sub-folders within this folder, which can be viewed by clicking it.

This needs practice. For example, if you click the **+** sign beside the **Survey** folder, you will see it expanded in the left-hand window, but it is not the selected folder so the right-hand pane will still show the contents of **GEA Marketing**, the selected folder.

Practise clicking the **+** and **–** signs beside various folders, and selecting folders and sub-folders, until you are clear about how the hierarchical structure works. Leave your screen looking like the one above for the next task.

Renaming a file

You can rename any file or folder.

Find **Letter**, right-click on it and select **Rename**.

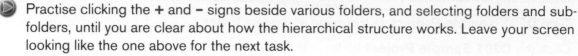

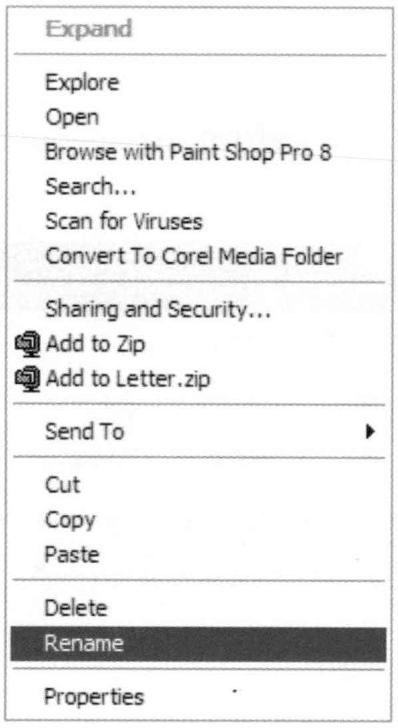

| Expand |
| Explore |
| Open |
| Browse with Paint Shop Pro 8 |
| Search... |
| Scan for Viruses |
| Convert To Corel Media Folder |
| Sharing and Security... |
| Add to Zip |
| Add to Letter.zip |
| Send To ▶ |
| Cut |
| Copy |
| Paste |
| Delete |
| Rename |
| Properties |

Figure 2.8

Change the folder name to **Letters** by editing the name and pressing **Enter**.

Copying and moving files and folders

You can copy a file to another folder or disk drive by first copying it to the **Clipboard**, and then pasting it to the desired location.

The **Clipboard** is a temporary storage area which holds the latest file or folder that you cut or copied. The next time you cut or copy something, the previous contents will be overwritten.

Suppose you have saved your project plan as **GEA Project Plan.doc** in the **My Documents** folder.

To copy it to the **Plan** folder:

- Select the file to be copied and click **Edit**, **Copy**. This copies the file to the **Clipboard**.
- In the left-hand window, click on the folder name **Plan** in **Epreparation**.
- Select **Edit**, **Paste**. The file will be copied to the **Plan** folder.

Now there are two copies of the file – one in the original location, and one in **Epreparation\Plan**.

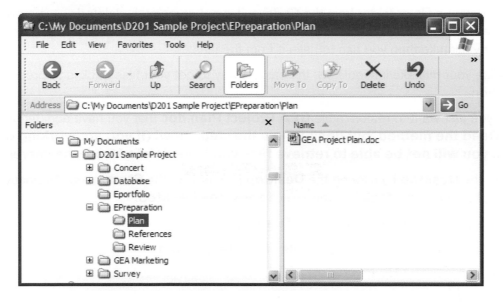

Figure 2.9

Note that folders can be copied in the same way. When you copy a folder, all its contents are copied too. You can also use this method to copy files or folders to another drive, such as the **A:** drive.

Making backup copies

Copying files for backup purposes is an essential skill for everyone using a computer! Sooner or later you will have a disaster, such as your hard disk crashing, your laptop being stolen, or your file being infected with a virus. That's when you will be glad you have a recent copy of your work on a floppy disk or Flash memory stick safely tucked away in your desk drawer at home.

Deleting files and folders

You can delete files and folders easily:

Delete

● Select the file or folder to be deleted.

● Press the **Delete** key on the keyboard, or the **Delete** button.

You will be asked to confirm that you want to delete the file. If you are sure you have selected the correct item, click **Yes**.

The Recycle Bin

When you delete a file or folder from the **C:** drive, it is not completely deleted – it is moved to a storage area called the **Recycle Bin**. This is very useful because it means that if you deleted the wrong file by mistake then you can retrieve it from the bin!

Undo

If you realise your mistake immediately, the easiest way to get your files back is to press the **Undo** button.

Suppose you just want to restore a file **GEA Project Plan.doc** that you have accidentally deleted. **Read the method, but don't follow the steps now! (If you are working on a network, you will not be able to retrieve files you have deleted from the server.)**

● Go to the **Desktop** by clicking the **Desktop** icon next to the **Start** menu. Alternatively, you can right-click in the **Task** bar and select **Show the Desktop**.

Recycle Bin

● Double-click the **Recycle Bin** on the **Desktop**.

● A window opens showing the contents of the **Recycle Bin**.

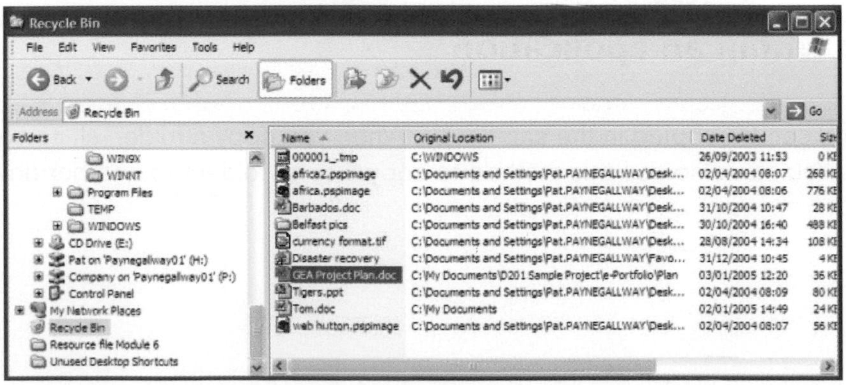

Figure 2.10

Right-click **GEA Project Plan.doc** and, from the pop-up menu, select **Restore**.

You can restore deleted folders in the same way.

Emptying the Recycle Bin

The contents of the **Recycle Bin** take up space on your hard disk. Although Windows will delete files from the **Recycle Bin** if it gets too big, it is a good idea to empty it now and then.

 On the **Desktop**, right-click the **Recycle Bin** and select **Empty Recycle Bin**. You will be asked to confirm your request. Remember, there is no getting those files back now!

Open
Browse with Paint Shop Pro 8
Explore
Empty Recycle Bin

Create Shortcut

Properties

Figure 2.11

Drag and drop

Another way of copying or moving files is to select them and then drag them to the new location.

Be aware of the following rule:

 Dragging a file or folder to a new location on the same drive **moves** the file or folder.

 Dragging a file or folder to a different drive **copies** the folder.

If you want to use drag and drop to copy a file to a new location on the same drive, hold down **Ctrl** while you drag.

Navigating within an application

Very often, within an application such as Word, you need to find a file, save a file in a particular folder, create a new folder or delete a file.

For example, suppose you want to open the file **GEA Project Plan.doc** in Word.

 Open Word. From the **File** menu select **Open**.

From here you can double-click the folder you want, or click the down-arrow in the **Look in** box to find the correct folder. You can back up through sub-folders using the **Up One Level** button (see Figure 2.12).

Note that you can create a new folder in this window by clicking the **New Folder** button. You can also delete a selected file or folder using either the **Delete** key or the **Delete** button in this window.

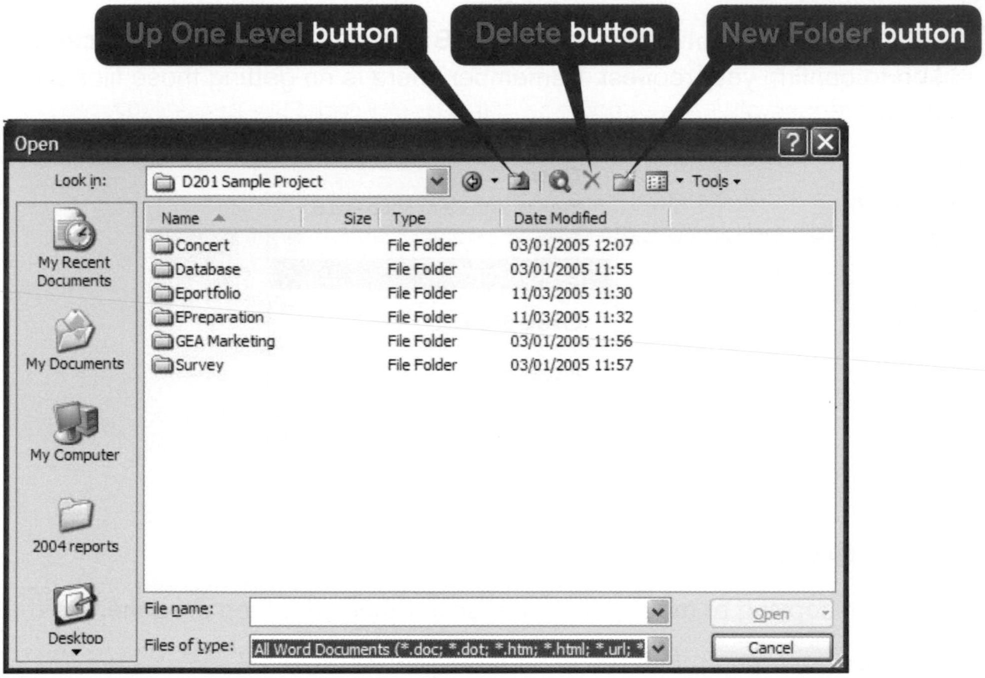

Figure 2.12

Windows Explorer

Another way of looking at and manipulating your files and folders is by using **Windows Explorer**.

Right-click the **Start** button and select **Explore**.

You will see a window similar to the one you opened from **My Computer**.

Now that you have created your folder structure, be sure to use it! Remember to keep early versions of each task so that you can show how the piece of work developed.

Chapter 3 – An Information Leaflet

For your eportfolio you will need to create an information leaflet using Publisher, Word or another application suitable for creating professional-looking brochures.

You must carry out your own research when you create your leaflet for the Edexcel SPB. Look at Section 2 for tips on doing research. The research for this leaflet has been based mainly on Internet resources, with a little more collected from WWF-UK. It is *very* important that you write down the source of everything that you use in creating your publications. This will give you an instant set of references at the end of the project rather than having to spend ages trying to track down where you got everything from.

This chapter will take you through the steps needed to create a three-panel leaflet for the GEA to help raise awareness of their cause and promote the work they are doing.

When you are creating your own leaflet it is a good idea to write down all the information you want to include in the publication and a description of what images you might like to add. With this, you can then produce a sketch of both sides of your proposed leaflet. It is not important to get a perfect drawing; just draw a rough outline of what bits could go where on the page. It is highly likely that you will end up making several changes to the design as you go along.

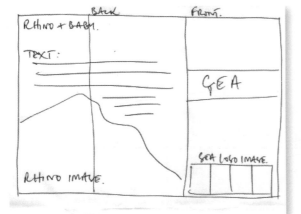

Tip:

Be careful to think about which panels of the page will end up where once you have folded it. Where you position the information will make a difference to the effectiveness of your leaflet.

Figure 3.1

Doing some preliminary research

Section 2 goes into some detail about how you should do your research, so you might like to look at some of this first. Otherwise, try looking for some images and text that you could use in the leaflet. Ask yourself what sort of things you would need to include in it and see what is available to help you.

You must acknowledge the source of everything that you use, so it would be a good idea to keep a notebook to record your sources in, or to create a new file in Word that you can keep adding to throughout the project.

▶ Load Word and enter a title at the top of the page saying **References:**

▶ Save this page as **References.doc** (in the folder called **References** under **Epreparation**). You will need to use it again later in this chapter, so don't close it yet.

Setting up a blank leaflet

▶ Open Publisher. You should see the **New Publication** task pane appear on the screen.

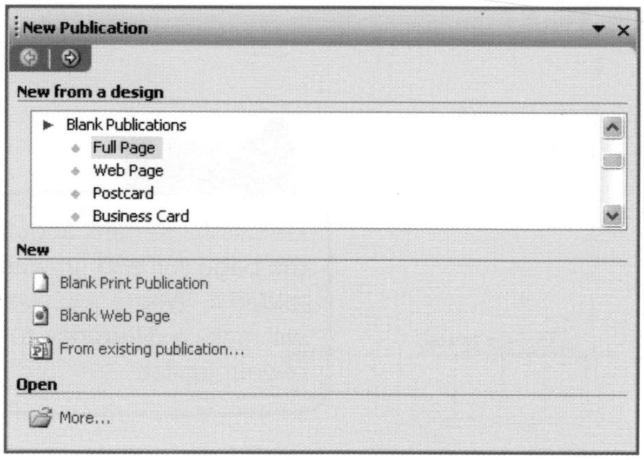

Figure 3.2

▶ Select **Blank Publications** in the **New from a design** list.

▶ Choose **Full Page** in the main window on the right.

▶ Click **File**, **Page Setup** on the main menu.

▶ Make sure that **Full Page** is selected and click the **Landscape** option.

▶ Click **OK**.

▶ Close the task pane.

You are aiming to produce an A4 leaflet that has two vertical folds, giving three panels of information. Publisher can provide guides to help you line up objects on the page.

▶ Click on **Arrange**, **Layout Guides** from the main menu.

▶ Reduce all of the **Margin Guides** to **0**.

▶ Select the **Grid Guides** tab and **3 Columns** by **1 Row**.

▶ Reduce the **Spacing** to **0.25cm**.

▶ Click the box to **Add center guide between columns and rows** and click **OK**.

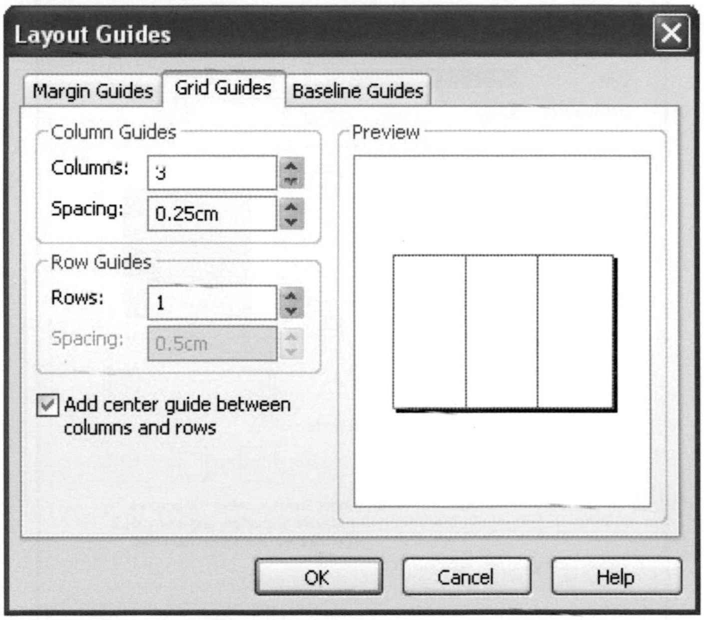

Layout Guides

| Margin Guides | Grid Guides | Baseline Guides |

Column Guides

Columns: 3

Spacing: 0.25cm

Row Guides

Rows: 1

Spacing: 0.5cm

☑ Add center guide between columns and rows

Preview

[OK] [Cancel] [Help]

Figure 3.3: Adjusting layout guides

This gives you the layout for the first page (one side of the whole leaflet).

▶ To get the second page, click **Insert**, **Page** on the menu.

▶ Select **1** new page and click **OK**.

▶ In the bottom left of the screen click on the **Page 1** icon to make sure that the first page is selected.

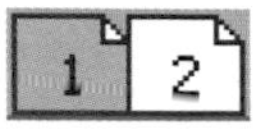

Page 1

Adding blocks of colour

Following a rough plan for the layout of the leaflet, the background and images will go in first, then the text can be fitted in around them.

Rectangle

◉ Use the **Rectangle** tool to draw a rectangle that covers the first two panels of the leaflet apart from a thin margin.

◉ Double-click the new rectangle and change its **Fill Color** to a rusty brown.

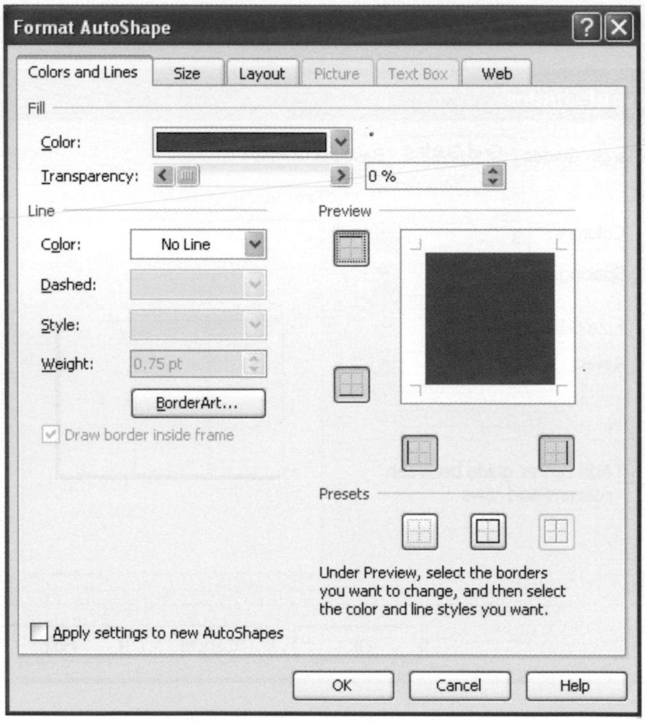

Figure 3.4

◉ Change the **Line Color** to **No Line**, then press **OK** to apply the new colour settings.

○ Add three more rectangles to the right-hand panel, and shade them in as shown in Figure 3.5. Leave space for an image to go in the middle.

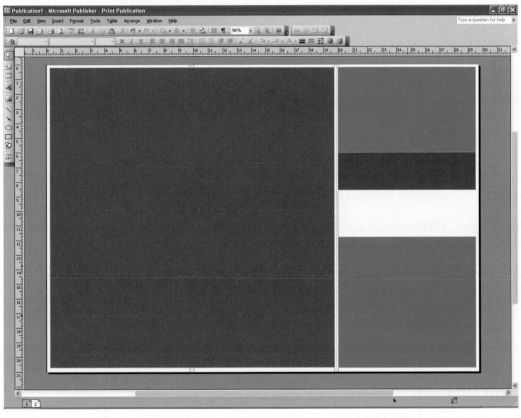

Figure 3.5

○ **Save** the leaflet so far as **GEALeaflet.pub**.

Selecting images

Now you can start adding some images. It is best to avoid clip art unless absolutely necessary. Clip art has no professional appeal and generally detracts from the final look you are trying to achieve. Photographic images are far preferable.

The images used in this example can be downloaded from the Payne-Gallway website at **www.payne-gallway.co.uk/didaD201**.

If you think carefully about the images you use, you could dramatically increase the effectiveness of your publication. Try going for emotion: horror, disgust and cute work very well! Just think of the horrific images you see at animal testing campaign stands in the high street. These include images of baby animals to help raise the readers' sympathy level immediately!

Recording your sources

When you find an image you are going to use, make sure you immediately copy the source of the picture into your **References** file in Word. You are about to use images of an orang-utan and a tiger in your leaflet.

All references need to be written in a particular way. Online images should follow the format:

> *Name of Picture*. **(Online image) Available** *http://www.web_address.com*, **Downloaded** *Date of document or, if not available, date of download*.

 Write down the following references in your **Reference** file:

> **Orang-utan baby. (Online image) Available http://www.payne-gallway.co.uk/ didaD201/Orangutan.jpg, Downloaded 30 November 2005.**
>
> **Bengal tiger. (Online image) Available http://www.payne-gallway.co.uk/ didaD201/BengalTiger.jpg, Downloaded 30 November 2005.**
>
> **GEA environment banner. (Online image) Available http://www.payne-gallway.co.uk/didaD201/GEA Environment.bmp, Downloaded 30 November 2005.**

 Save the **References** file again.

Inserting images

 Return to your Publisher leaflet.

 Select **Insert**, **Picture**, **From File**.

 Choose **Orangutan.jpg** and click **Insert**.

 Resize the image by dragging one of the corner handles. Do not use one of the handles in the middle of an edge, since this would make the image distort and stretch which looks very unprofessional and could lose you marks.

 Position the picture in the top left of the page so that it fits in between the blue layout guides visible round the edge between the first and second columns.

 If the **Picture** toolbar is not already visible, right-click the image and select **Show Picture Toolbar**.

Set Transparent Color

 Select the **Set Transparent Color** tool and click the white area.

Tip:

These images have already been manipulated slightly using Adobe Photoshop to get the white area a pure white. You can do the same to your images by using the Magic Wand tool in Photoshop (or a similar graphics package) and shading in the selected area with a white brush.

- Insert the **BengalTiger.jpg** and **GEA Environment.bmp** images into the spaces shown in Figure 3.6.

- Make the tiger's white background transparent.

- Use the **Crop** tool on the **Picture** toolbar to cut off the tiger's tail. Be careful! Line it up with the edge of the rusty-coloured area.

Crop

Figure 3.6: Using the Crop tool

Adding text boxes

The right-hand panel will become the front page when it is all folded up, so you need to put the GEA's name on it. It is a common mistake to dive in and go for a piece of WordArt for a title or important heading, but in professional publications WordArt is seldom used, because it can look very tacky. It is best to avoid it; use a normal font and just increase the size.

⊚ Select the **Text Box** tool and draw a box in the top right of the page.

⊚ Use the **Formatting** toolbar to change the font to **Arial**, size **90** (hint: type this – it's not in the drop-down list), **Centred** and **White**.

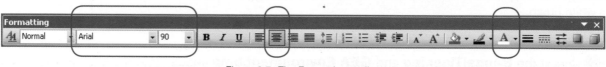

Figure 3.7: The Formatting toolbar

To keep the look of the leaflet consistent, use only a very small number of different styles.

⊚ Add another text box directly underneath. Make the text **Arial**, size **24**, **Centred** and change the colour to **Dark Green**. Type the text **Global Environment Association**.

⊚ Add another text box with the GEA's slogan in green at the bottom of the panel (see Figure 3.8).

Figure 3.8: Adding text boxes

Recording your development

It is important to be able to show the sequence of development during the creation of the leaflet and the other components of the project. To do this, save regularly under different filenames that change in version number.

 Save the leaflet again, as **GEALeaflet v1.pub**.

You can also use these versions to show how your ideas changed and how mistakes were corrected as you went along.

Adding blocks of text

 Now add two more text boxes with the following information about tigers and orang-utans. Make the font style for the headings **Arial**, size **20** in **White**; the rest of the text should be **Arial**, size **12** in **Black**.

Tigers

Of the eight sub-species of tiger, there are only 5 still in existence today. Over the last century numbers have fallen from around 100,000 to only 5,000. They are constantly under threat from poachers, and their natural habitats are shrinking owing to human interference. The GEA has been working for years to raise funds to try to reduce such threats and sustain tiger numbers in the wild.

Orang-utans

This baby orang-utan is one of several protected by the GEA, however many of the remaining population in Malaysia are seen as pets. The pet trade is responsible for killing mothers in order to get to their young. It is estimated that in recent years 10,000 of the great apes have been killed in order to supply 2,000 babies as pets to Taiwan.

Orang-utans eat both plants and small mammals, however their favourite food is fruit. They spend their entire lives high in the trees of the Malaysian forest. They are solitary animals, spending nearly their entire adult life alone. Each male has a large territory which overlaps several female territories. Their territories are very large and operations by logging companies and large commercial plantations threaten to reduce the size of their forest habitat.

 Position the tiger information to the left of the tiger. The information about the orang-utan can go above the tiger.

 Place another small text box (**Arial**, size **12** and **Centred**) just above the tiger's back and type in '**Do you think that endangered animals should be kept as pets?**'

Use the **AutoShapes** tool to place a **Rounded Rectangle** over the text box. You'll find the **Rounded Rectangle** under **Basic Shapes**.

Right-click the rounded rectangle and select **Format AutoShape**. Fill the shape with a **Muddy Brown** colour, giving it an **Orange** border with a **Line Weight** of **2 pt**.

Right-click the shape and select **Order**, **Send Backward**.

Your finished page should look like the one below.

Figure 3.9: The first page

Now you need to complete the reverse side of the leaflet, shown in Figure 3.10. All the skills needed are the same but you can complete it to practise what you have learnt in producing this side of the leaflet.

Save the leaflet as **GEALeaflet v2.pub**.

The files you will need are also downloadable from the Payne-Gallway website. They are called **RhinoAndBaby.jpg** and **GoldenEagle.jpg**.

All of the fonts and sizes match those used on the first side in order to maintain a consistent style. This is important for high marks.

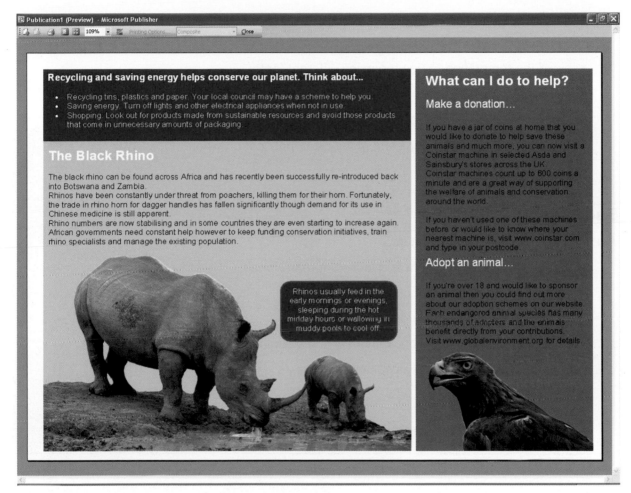

Figure 3.10: The reverse side of the leaflet

Finish the reverse side of the leaflet and save the final completed version as **GEALeaflet. pub**. This will overwrite the original version.

Good marks... ✓

You will get good marks for your leaflet if you:

- use a suitable structure and style for the leaflet;
- avoid clip art and WordArt;
- avoid the temptation to use too many different fonts;
- make sure the style of presentation is suitable for the target audience;
- check your publications for accuracy (spell check AND proofread!);
- ask others for their opinions and modify your publication where necessary;
- acknowledge copyright.

Bad marks... ✗

You will lose marks for your leaflet if:

- your work is not consistent and looks unprofessional;
- you use irrelevant images or content;
- you don't spell check or proofread your work;
- you use other people's work without acknowledging them;
- your work looks the same as someone else's.

Chapter 4 – Using Surveys

Surveys are used to gather information from people, and can be used to find out, for example:

- people's opinions;
- their likes and dislikes;
- what type of person or age group is most likely to buy a particular product;
- how much they will be prepared to spend;
- when they are most likely to make a purchase.

An environmental organisation such as GEA could design a questionnaire to find out people's views on endangered species. Here is part of a questionnaire:

National Survey 2005

Q1   Do you think it matters if a species becomes extinct?

Yes, a lot ☐   Yes, a little ☐   Not really ☐

Q2   Do you care more about wildlife in the UK or overseas?

In the UK ☐   Overseas ☐   Both the same ☐

Q3   Tiger bones and rhino horn are used in traditional oriental medicine and the species are facing extinction as a result. Do you think their use is justified?

Yes ☐

Yes, because people are entitled to their own cultural beliefs ☐

No ☐

Q4   People support our organisation for a number of reasons. Please tell us which area of work is of most interest to you. (Tick one)

Protecting endangered species	☐
Protecting the environment	☐
Campaigning on environmental issues	☐
Working with communities to promote sustainable livelihoods	☐

By answering these questions you can help us plan future fundraising campaigns that may be of interest to you.

Is your age?

Under 18 ☐	18-25 ☐	26-35 ☐
36-50 ☐	51-70 ☐	Over 70 ☐

Are you?   Male ☐   Female ☐

Figure 4.1

If you are planning to do a survey, you must design questionnaires that:

- collect all the data you need;
- do not influence the responses people give;
- record the data in a format that is easy to analyse;
- are easy to complete.

Questions:

1. **What is the purpose of the questionnaire shown in Figure 4.1?**
2. **What information is the organisation trying to find out?**
3. **Are the questions unambiguous?**
4. **Why are there questions about the age and sex of the respondents?**

Gathering the information

Once you have designed your questionnaire, you must find a way of getting people to answer it. You might consider one of the following ways:

- posting the questionnaire to your mailing list of supporters;
- emailing the questionnaire to supporters;
- asking people in a shopping mall to complete the questionnaire;
- telephoning people in a particular area to ask them the questions.

Question:

What are the advantages and disadvantages of each of these methods?

Asking the right people

You might get completely different answers to the questions, depending on when and where you carry out the survey. For example, if you send the questionnaire to people who already support the environmental organisation you may get different answers from those you get if you give the questionnaire to people in the street.

Supposing you wanted to find out how many people in the UK felt that there was too much football shown on TV. You would get very different responses if you handed out the questionnaires at a football match, or in an old people's home.

Therefore, you must select your group of respondents very carefully if you want to ensure that the answers accurately reflect the views of the population as a whole.

How many people?

Obviously, it is impossible to survey everyone in the population. Businesses and other organisations have to decide how they are going to get a reasonable number of responses from a section of the population, chosen to represent the views of the population as a whole. There are different methods of choosing a sample to survey:

- **Random sampling**. A percentage of the population in a particular area is interviewed, with each person in the area having an equal chance of being approached. Up to 5–10% of the population in the area may be interviewed to get an accurate reflection of the views of the whole population.

- **Quota sampling**. The population is split into segments according to age, sex, income or other criteria, and the number of people interviewed in each segment reflects the make-up of the whole population. For example if 15% of the population are between 18 and 25 then 15% of the total number of people surveyed must fit this category.

- **Targeted sampling**. The sample may be chosen by geographical area. For example, if an entrepreneur is gathering information on prospective customers before opening up a sandwich shop in the local High Street, he might sample as many people as possible on the street to find out whether they would be likely to come into his shop.

Practical work: creating a questionnaire

You are going to use Word to create the questionnaire shown in Figure 4.1. You will learn to:

- set margins and tabs;
- use formatting styles;
- change line spacing;
- Insert special symbols.

For the Edexcel SPB you will probably have to design a questionnaire; this could be done in Word, Publisher or even Excel. Possibly it could form part of a leaflet.

Remember to save different versions of your questionnaire as you develop and change it in response to user feedback. You will need to show development work in your eportfolio. Use sensible filenames and save your work in an appropriate folder, which you should have already set up for this purpose.

Setting the margins in a new document

 Open a new document in Word.

 From the menu, select **File**, **Page Setup**. You will see the following screen:

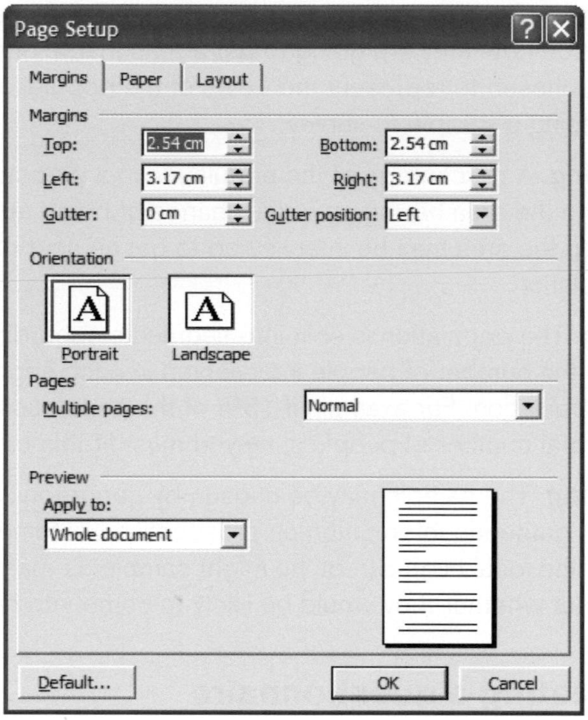

Figure 4.2: Setting margins in a Word document

 Set the **Top** margin to **4 cm**, and the three other margins to **2.5 cm**. Then click **OK**.

Using existing styles

Word uses styles to group together text settings such as font name and paragraph spacing. This makes it easy to change the formatting of text: just apply the new style. If you modify a style, for example by making it bold, then all of the text that has that style will be automatically updated with the new settings.

For the heading you can use one of Word's built-in styles, called **Heading 1**.

 On the **Formatting** toolbar, click the down-arrow in the **Style** box.

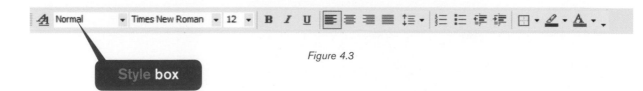

Figure 4.3

▶ Select **Heading 1** from the drop-down list of styles.

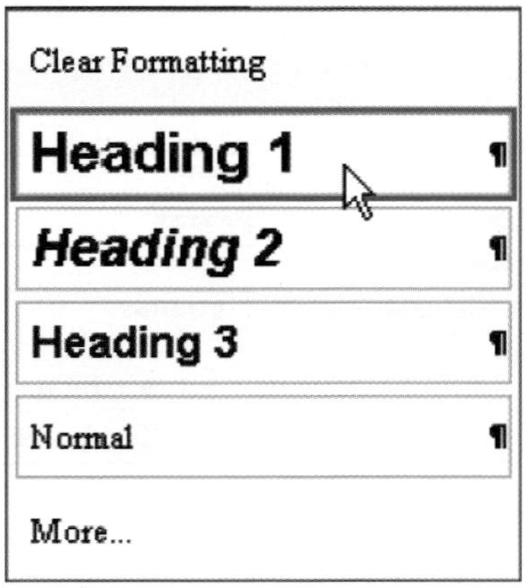

Figure 4.4

▶ Enter the text **National Survey 2005** and press **Enter** twice. Notice that the style box now says **Normal**, because that is the style which by default will follow **Heading 1**.

Creating a new style

We will create a new style for the questions. The new style will use Arial font, size 12 and will have a 'hanging indent' so that text lines up neatly.

▶ Type the following text (press the **Tab** key after **Q1**):
   Q1   Do you think it matters if a species becomes extinct?

▶ From the **Format** menu select **Styles and Formatting**. You will see a **Task pane** appear on the right of the screen.

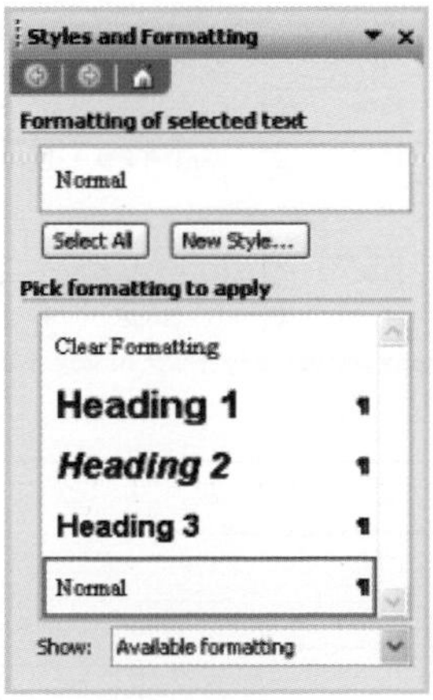

Figure 4.5

○ Click the **New Style** button.

○ In the **New Style** window, give the style the name. Set the font to **Arial**, size **12**.

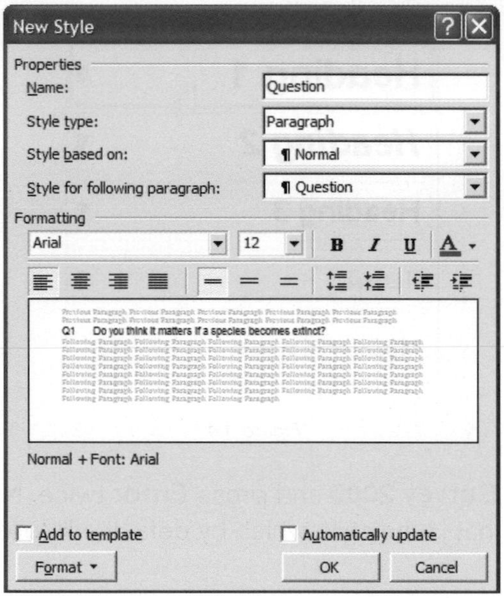

Figure 4.6

○ Click the **Format** button in this window and select **Paragraph**. Create a **Hanging indent** at **1 cm** and increase the **Spacing After** to **6 pt**, as in Figure 4.7.

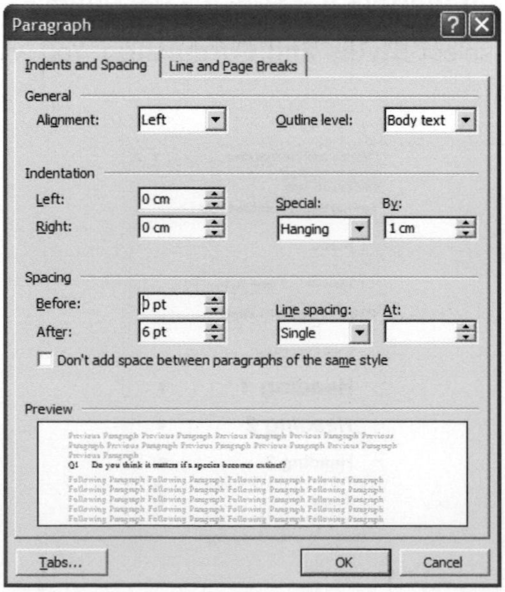

Figure 4.7

- Click **OK**, and **OK** in the next window.

- Click anywhere in the question text, and then click in the **Style** box to select your new **Question** style. Press **Enter**.

- Next, create a style called **Response**. It should be based on **Question**, have the **Response** style for the following paragraph, and have a **Left indent** of **1cm** with no **Hanging indent**.

- Type the words **Yes, a lot** and then apply your new **Response** style to them.

Inserting a special symbol

Next you need to insert the little square for people to tick.

- From the **Insert** menu select **Symbol**.

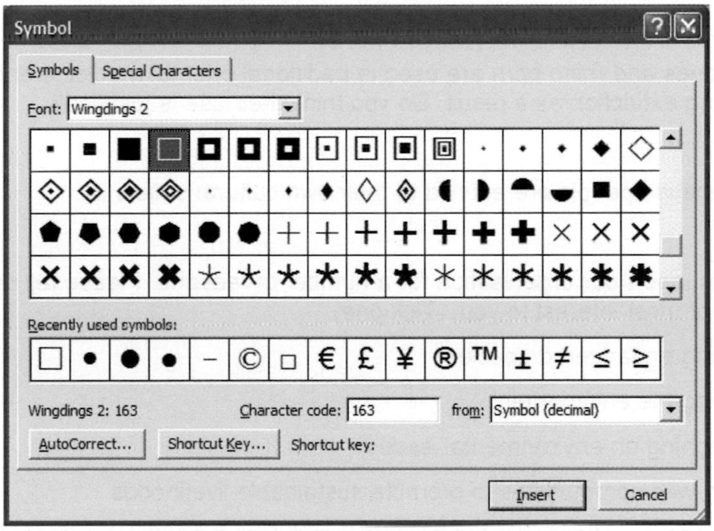

Figure 4.8

- Change the **Font** to **Wingdings 2**.

- Find the square, select it and click **Insert**.

- Use the **Tab** key to tab across, and type in the rest of the line. You should always use tabs rather than spaces to ensure that text lines up properly.

You can finish the questionnaire on your own, and save it in the **Survey** folder. In your project work for the Edexcel SPB, the next step would be to get at least fifty copies of your questionnaire filled in. You may be able to work in a group to achieve this – ask your teacher for advice.

As this is just a practice run, you do not need to conduct a real survey for this exercise. In the next chapter, you will be given the results of the survey to analyse.

Analysing data from a survey

Once you have collected the responses from a survey, the next step is to analyse them so that you can extract useful information about the population you have surveyed.

Suppose that you are given a number of completed survey forms to analyse. You are expected to interpret the information you extract and to select and present the information clearly.

A typical completed form looks like this:

National Survey 2005

Q1   Do you think it matters if a species becomes extinct?

   Yes, a lot ☒   Yes, a little ☐   Not really ☐

Q2   Do you care more about wildlife in the UK or overseas?

   In the UK ☐   Overseas ☐   Both the same ☒

Q3   Tiger bones and rhino horn are used in traditional oriental medicine and the species are facing extinction as a result. Do you think their use is justified?

   Yes ☐

   Yes, because people are entitled to their own cultural beliefs ☐

   No ☒

Q4   People support our organisation for a number of reasons. Please tell us which area of work is of most interest to you. (Tick one)

   Protecting endangered species   ☐

   Protecting the environment   ☒

   Campaigning on environmental issues   ☐

   Working with communities to promote sustainable livelihoods   ☐

By answering these questions you can help us plan future fundraising campaigns that may be of interest to you.

Is your age?

   Under 18 ☒   18-25 ☐   26-35   ☐

   36-50   ☐   51-70 ☐   Over 70 ☐

Are you?   Male ☒   Female ☐

Figure 5.1

Analysing responses

In order to analyse the responses, you must think about what information you are hoping to extract. Here are some examples of questions that you may be able to answer with the help of the questionnaire responses:

1   What percentage of the population surveyed think it matters a lot if a species becomes extinct?

2   What percentage of people care more about wildlife in the UK than overseas?

Question:

What other questions can be answered with the help of the questionnaire responses?

Look at the last two questions on the questionnaire. They are included because it may be useful for the charity to know whether the opinions of people under 18, for example, are different from those of people in other age groups.

Question:

Why might it be useful to know whether the opinions of people under 18 are different from those of people in other age groups?

Practical work: Using a spreadsheet

A spreadsheet is a very useful tool for analysing data and presenting information clearly. The first step is to think about how you are going to lay out the spreadsheet. Then you can enter the raw data ready for analysis.

You will learn how to:

- design the layout of a spreadsheet;
- enter, cut, copy, paste and move data;
- format cells;
- insert/delete rows/columns;
- enter formulae;
- sort data;
- test your spreadsheet;
- interpret the information provided by the spreadsheet.

There are many possible ways of laying out the spreadsheet to hold the survey results, and you will need to experiment to find the best way. Partly this will depend on the number of questions in the survey, and the nature of the questions.

Here is one possible way of laying out the spreadsheet. Some data has already been entered in the nine visible rows (Row 7 to Row 15). Only two of the questions have been entered in the spreadsheet shown in Figure 5.2.

	A	B	C	D	E	F	G	H	I	J	K
1											
2											
3											
4	1	Do you think it matters if a species becomes extinc					2	Care more about UK or overseas?			
5											
6		A lot	A little	Not really				UK		Overseas	Same
7	1	1								1	
8	2			1						1	
9	3	1								1	
10	4	1						1			
11	5		1								1
12	6	1								1	
13	7	1								1	
14	8	1									1
15	9		1							1	

Sheet1 / Sheet2 / Sheet3 /

Figure 5.2

Entering the survey questions

Bold

Font Color

▶ Open a new spreadsheet in Excel.

▶ Enter all of the text shown in Figure 5.2.

▶ Click in the row header for row 4. Use the **Bold** button to make the text bold, and the **Font Color** button to make the text blue.

▶ Make the text in row 6 bold and blue. Repeat for column A.

Formatting the text

All the text in row 6 needs to be right-aligned so that it is over the numbers.

Align Right

Merge and Center

▶ Click row header 6 to select the row. Then click the **Align Right** button.

We will make the text of Question 1 wrap across cells B4 to D4.

▶ Select cells B4 to D4, and click the **Merge and Center** button. The text will not fit in this space, and needs to 'wrap'.

▶ With cells B4 to D4 still selected, select **Format, Cells** from the main menu. Click the **Alignment** tab.

▶ Click the **Wrap text** option.

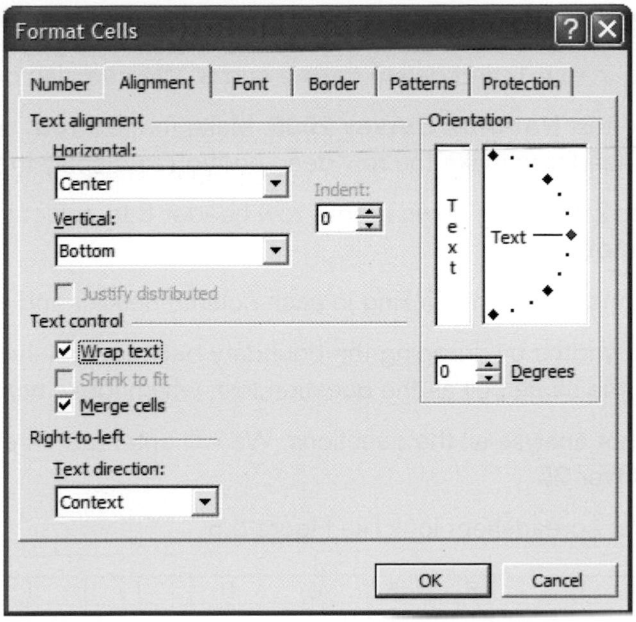

Figure 5.3

▶ Click **OK**.

The row is not deep enough for all the text to show.

▶ Drag the boundary between row headers 4 and 5 down until the row is as deep as three regular rows. This will allow space for longer questions.

▶ Now do the same for Question 2. Your spreadsheet should look like Figure 5.4.

	A	B	C	D	E	F	G	H	I	J	K
1											
2											
3											
4	1	Do you think it matters if a species becomes extinct?					2	Care more about UK or overseas?			
5											
6		A lot	A little	Not really					UK	Overseas	Same	
7	1	1								1		
8	2			1						1		
9	3	1								1		
10	4	1							1			
11	5		1								1	
12	6	1								1		
13	7	1								1		

Sheet1 / Sheet2 / Sheet3 /

Figure 5.4

Deleting rows and columns

We will insert a heading in row 1, and delete rows 2 and 3. We can also delete columns E and F.

 In cell A1, write the text **National Survey 2005**. Make the text **red**, size **18**. You may need to click in the row header to make the row deep enough to display the text.

 Click in row header 2 and drag down across row header 3 to select both rows. Then right-click and select **Delete**.

 Delete columns E and F by right-clicking in each column header and selecting **Delete**.

You can change column widths by dragging the boundary between column headers. You can put the question number in the same cell as the question text, which looks neater.

In this example we will not analyse all the questions. We will enter just three age groups: Under 18, 18–25 and Over 25.

See if you can make your spreadsheet look like Figure 5.5.

	A	B	C	D	E	F	G	H	I	J	K	L
1	National Survey 2005											
2		1. Do you think it matters if a species becomes extinct?				2. Care more about UK or overseas?				Age group		
3												
4		A lot	A little	Not really		UK	Overseas	Same		Under 18	18-25	Over 25
5	1	1						1		1		
6	2			1				1		1		
7	3	1						1			1	
8	4	1				1				1		
9	5		1						1			1
10	6	1						1				1
11	7	1						1				1
12	8	1							1			1
13	9		1					1				1

Sheet1 / Sheet2 / Sheet3 /

Figure 5.5

Copying and pasting a series

In column A, you can automatically extend the sequence of numbers:

 Select cells A12 and A13. Drag the corner handle down the column to row 81. This fills the column with consecutive numbers.

Undo

Try pressing the **Undo** button and experimenting by selecting only cell A13, and dragging its corner handle. What happens?

When you have finished experimenting you can restore your list of consecutive numbers. You will need somewhere between 50 and 100 responses to perform a realistic analysis. You can enter your own data, or you can download the file **Survey Method1.xls** from the website **www.payne-gallway.co.uk/didaD201**. This file has 75 responses.

Analysing the data

We can start by doing some simple analysis of how many people, and what percentage of the total surveyed, fit into each category: care a lot if a species becomes extinct, for example. Since there is quite a lot of data to analyse, we need to keep the headings visible on the screen even when we scroll down. To do this you need to **freeze panes**.

Freezing panes

With the cursor in cell B5, select **Window**, **Freeze Panes** from the main menu.

Scroll down to the bottom of the spreadsheet. The titles remain in view. Notice that in this spreadsheet, the total number surveyed (75) has been inserted in cell J1. We will be calculating totals in row 81 and percentages in row 82.

	A	B	C	D	E	F	G	H	I	J	K	L
1	**National Survey 2005**						Total number surveyed:			75		
2		1. Do you think it matters if a species becomes extinct?					2. Care more about UK or overseas?			Age group		
3												
4		A lot	A little	Not really			UK	Overseas	Same	Under 18	18-25	Over 25
70	66	1						1				1
71	67	1					1				1	
72	68	1					1				1	
73	69			1			1				1	
74	70	1					1				1	
75	71	1						1		1		
76	72	1						1		1		
77	73	1						1			1	
78	74		1					1				1
79	75	1						1			1	
80												
81	Total											
82	Percentage of total											
83												

Sheet1 / Sheet2 / Sheet3 /

Figure 5.6

Calculating and copying totals and percentages

Σ

AutoSum

▶ With the cursor in cell B81, click the **AutoSum** button. Then drag the corner of the selection up to cell B5. Press **Enter**, and the formula **=SUM(B5:B80)** is automatically entered in cell B81. You could, of course, type this formula in the cell yourself.

▶ To copy this formula to cells C81 and D81, click in the cell and drag the corner handle across cells C81 and D81.

▶ With the three cells selected, right-click and select **Copy**. Then right-click in cell F81 and select **Paste**. Right-click in cell J81 and select **Paste**.

▶ Press **Esc** to get rid of the 'marching ants' round the copied cells.

In cell B82, we will enter a formula for the percentage of respondents; that is, the total in cell B81 as a percentage of the total number surveyed.

We have to be careful here, because when we copy and paste the formula to other cells, we want the total number surveyed to always refer to cell B3 – in other words, this is an **absolute reference**. An absolute reference is denoted by a **$** sign in front of the column letter and row number, such as in **B3**.

▶ In cell B82, type an **=** sign and then click in cell B81. Type a **/** symbol and click in cell J1.

▶ Now you can press the shortcut key **F4** to turn the cell reference J1 from a **relative** to an **absolute** reference.

▶ Type a **%** sign (hold down **Shift** and press **5**) and then press **Enter**. This tells you that 65.33% of people surveyed care a lot if a species becomes extinct. (The data is made up, so don't quote these figures!)

▶ Copy this cell to the other cells as shown in Figure 5.7.

79		75	1						1			1
80												
81	Total	49	15	11		20	30	25		29	23	23
82	Percentage of total	65.33	20	14.666667		27	40	33.33		38.66667	30.66667	30.66667
83												
84												

Sheet1 / Sheet2 / Sheet3 /

Select destination and press ENTER or choose Paste   Sum=100   NUM

Figure 5.7

Sum of selected cells shown here

Checking your results

It is very important to check that your results are reasonable. In this case, the total of cells J82, K82 and L82 should be exactly 100. To check that this is so, highlight the three cells. The sum of the highlighted cells appears in the **Status** bar – this is a very useful feature!

Formatting numbers

You should format each of the cells in row 82. One decimal place is sufficient – or even no decimal places, as the survey only takes in a small sample of the population and cannot represent with total accuracy the views of everyone in the country.

 Select cells B82 to L82.

 From the main menu select **Format**, **Cells**.

 Click the **Number** tab and select category **Number**.

 Set the number of decimal places to **0** and click **OK**.

 Notice that if you highlight cells J82 to L82, the **Sum** in the **Status** bar still says **100**, even though the numbers appear to add up to 101. This is because, although the numbers are displayed as whole numbers, the computer holds them to a much higher degree of accuracy.

Filtering data

We can do a more complex analysis on the data to find out if the views of people in different age groups differ.

First of all, we will filter out the **Under 18** age group.

 Put the cursor in cell J5. Then select **Data**, **Filter**, **Autofilter** from the main menu.

 Select **1** from the drop-down list in cell J4.

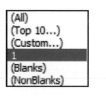

Figure 5.8

There are 29 under 18s in the survey. However, cells B81, C81 and D81 still show the totals for the whole set of 75 responses. We want a subtotal for the relevant age group.

Insert function

⊘ Delete the contents of cells B81 to D81.

⊘ Click in cell B81 and then click the **Insert function** button in the **Formula bar**.

⊘ Make sure **All** is selected in the category box, and then scroll down the list of functions to select **SUBTOTAL**.

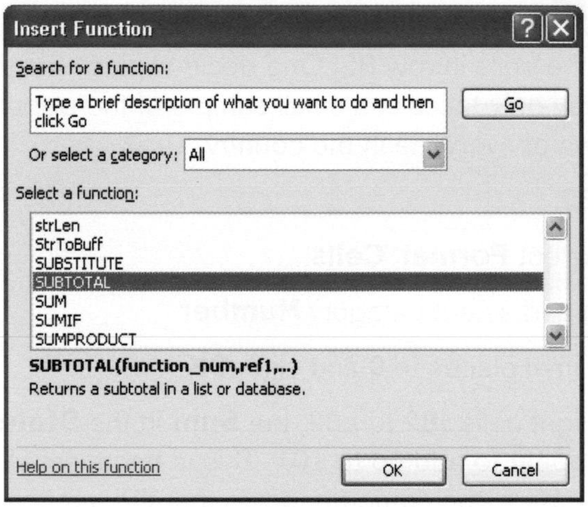

Insert Function   [?] [X]

Search for a function:

| Type a brief description of what you want to do and then click Go | Go |

Or select a category: All ▾

Select a function:

strLen
StrToBuff
SUBSTITUTE
SUBTOTAL
SUM
SUMIF
SUMPRODUCT

SUBTOTAL(function_num,ref1,...)
Returns a subtotal in a list or database.

Help on this function   [OK]   [Cancel]

Figure 5.9

⊘ Click **OK**.

⊘ You can get help on this function by clicking **Help on this function** at the bottom of the screen. The following information is displayed:

SUBTOTAL(function_num, ref1, ref2,...)

Function_num is the number 1 to 11 that specifies which function to use in calculating subtotals within a list.

Function_Num	Function
1	AVERAGE
2	COUNT
3	COUNTA
4	MAX
5	MIN
6	PRODUCT
7	STDEV
8	STDEVP
9	SUM
10	VAR
11	VARP

Figure 5.10

We want a **SUM** subtotal, so the **function_num** is **9**. **Ref1** is the range that is to be summed.

 Fill in the window as shown below:

Function Arguments		⊠
SUBTOTAL		
Function_num	9	= 9
Ref1	B5:B79	= {1;0;1;1;0;1;1;1;0;1
Ref2		= reference
		= 20

Returns a subtotal in a list or database.

Ref1: ref1,ref2,... are 1 to 29 ranges or references for which you want the subtotal.

Formula result =   20

Help on this function   OK   Cancel

Figure 5.11

 Click **OK**.

The total of the subset selected by the filter is shown; in this case, the 20 under 18s who think extinction matters a lot.

 Copy the formula from cell B81 to the other cells in the same row (see Figure 5.12).

 Add new headings as shown in Figure 5.12; we will copy the values for each age group to the new locations.

		1. Do you think it matters if a species becomes extinct?				2. Care more about UK or overseas?				Age group		
2												
3												
4		A lot	A little	Not really		UK	Overseas	Same		Under ▼	18- ▼	Over ▼
75	71	1					1			1		
76	72	1						1		1		
80												
81	Total	20	3	6		8	15	6		29	0	0
82	Percentage of total	27	4	8		11	20	8		39	0	0
83												
84	**Under 18**											
85	Total											
86	Percentage of total											
87												
88	**18-25 age group**											
89	Total											
90	Percentage of total											
91												
92	**Over 25**											
93	Total											
94	Percentage of total											
95												

Figure 5.12

Paste Special

We want to copy the values, not the formulae, to Row 85 for the Under 18s. You will see why in a moment.

Copy

▶ Select cells B81 to H81 and click the **Copy** button.

▶ Place the cursor in cell B85 and from the main menu select **Edit**, **Paste Special**.

▶ Select **Values** in the dialogue box (Figure 5.13) and click **OK**.

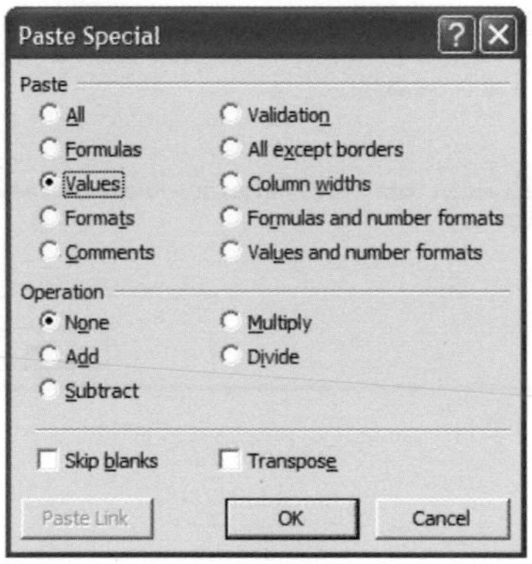

Figure 5.13

Finishing the analysis

Now you need to remove the filter in the **Under 18** column, and put a filter on the **18-25** age group.

▶ Click the down-arrow in cell J4 and select **(All)** from the drop-down list.

▶ Click the down-arrow in cell K4 and select **1**.

Notice that the totals in row 81 have changed. That is why you needed to copy the values, not the formulae, to row 85.

▶ Copy cells B81 to H81 and paste their values into row 89.

▶ Now repeat these steps to get the totals for the over 25 age group.

▶ Change the filter so that all of the results are shown.

▶ Calculate the percentage in cell B86. The formula is **=B85/J81%**.

Fill in the rest of the formulae to complete the spreadsheet. You should get the following results:

	A	B	C	D	E	F	G	H	I	J	K	L
1	**National Survey 2005**						Total number surveyed:			75		
2		**1. Do you think it matters if a species becomes extinct?**					**2. Care more about UK or overseas?**			**Age group**		
3												
4		A lot	A little	Not really		UK	Overseas	Same		Under ▼	18- ▼	Over ▼
75	71	1						1		1		
76	72	1							1	1		
77	73	1							1		1	
78	74		1						1			1
79	75	1							1		1	
80												
81	Total	49	15	11		20	30	25		29	23	23
82	Percentage of total	65	20	15		27	40	33		39	31	31
83												
84	**Under 18**											
85	Total	20	3	6		8	15	6				
86	Percentage of total	69	10	21		28	52	21				
87												
88	**18-25 age group**											
89	Total	16	5	2		5	8	10				
90	Percentage of total	70	22	9		22	35	43				
91												
92	**Over 25**											
93	Total	13	7	3		7	7	9				
94	Percentage of total	57	30	13		30	30	39				

Figure 5.14

Interpreting the information

Well done! You have performed quite a thorough analysis of the survey results. But what does it all mean? Can you draw any conclusions? How will the results help in planning future fundraising campaigns?

Questions:

Looking at the totals and percentages, see if you can answer the following questions.

1. **What percentage of the population surveyed thinks that it does not matter if a species becomes extinct?**

2. **What percentage of under 18s thinks that it does not matter if a species becomes extinct?**

3. **What percentage of the population surveyed cares more about wildlife in the UK than overseas?**

4. **Is the under 18 age group typical of the whole population in their answers to Question 2 of the survey? ("Do you care more about wildlife in the UK or overseas?")**

These are the sort of questions that you should be able to answer once you have performed your analysis. The next stage is to present your results in a way that is clear and easy to understand. We'll look at ways of doing this in the next chapter.

▶ Save your spreadsheet as **Survey Method1**, in the **Survey\Analysis** folder.

Charts can be extremely useful, as they often make pages of data easier to understand. A suitable chart can help to show at a glance which products or which holiday months are most popular, or whether figures such as sales or exam results are better or worse than in previous years. A chart can be used to show a trend or to forecast figures into the future.

There are several types of chart that you can choose from, including line chart, bar chart and pie chart. Different types of chart are appropriate in different circumstances, and you cannot choose an exploding doughnut chart just because it looks pretty! The question is, does it make the data clearer than a table of figures?

Here is an example of a completely wrong use of a type of pie chart.

Example 1

Average temperatures in Barcelona: January 10°C, February 13°C, March 13°C, April 14°C, May 18°C, June 21°C, July 25°C, August 25°C, September 22°C, October 18°C, November 16°C, December 12°C.

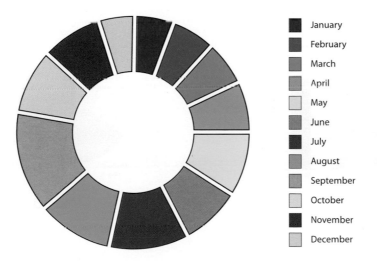

Figure 6.1: Inappropriate use of a type of pie chart

Now what information does this chart convey? Absolutely none! Even if you add numbers, it is a totally inappropriate chart.

Tip:

Never use a pie chart except to show parts of a whole. Conversely, **never** use a line graph to show parts of a whole. Always think about the purpose of the chart.

Question:

What type of chart would be more appropriate, and why?

Example 2

A company has five different products, and has calculated the profit on each. You are required to show these figures in a suitable chart.

Product	Profit in £000s
Model A	12.57
Model B	4.60
Model C	6.50
Model D	1.34
Model E	10.24

Questions:

Which of the charts below is most suitable? Which is totally unsuitable? Why? How could the more suitable charts be improved? What is a 'legend' used for?

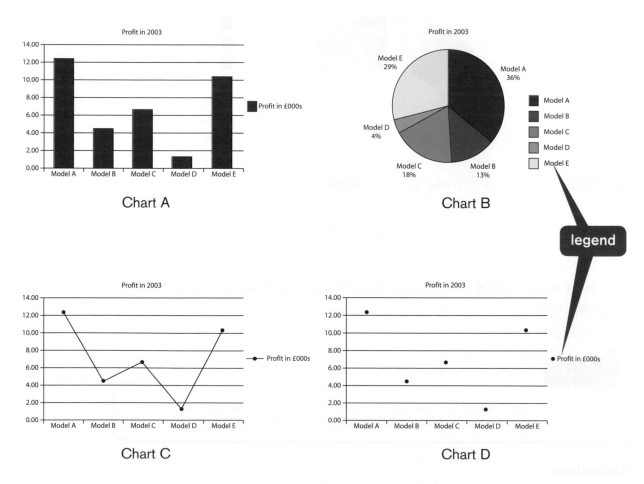

Figure 6.2: Possible chart types for showing profits

Answer:

The pie chart is a good one for this situation, as it shows at a glance that Models A and E bring in about two-thirds of the total profit. The bar chart is also quite suitable, as it shows clearly which are the most profitable products, though it is not quite as informative as the pie chart. The line chart is totally unsuitable. Line charts are used to show a trend over time – for example your height as you grow, your weight as you go on a diet, or the sales for each month of a year. In this example we could easily switch the order of the products and then the line would have a completely different shape, which is very misleading. Chart D is neither attractive nor informative – you're better off with the original table of figures.

The pie chart could be made even more informative by including the actual profit figures as well as the percentages. Both the bar chart and the pie chart could have a bigger, bolder title. The bar chart could have a Y-axis label to say that the axis represents thousands of pounds.

The legend (or key) is used to show what the bars or pie slices represent.

Tip:

You must make sure your chart is 'fit for purpose' – you will get no credit for an inappropriate chart.

In this chapter we will take the summary data from the survey and present it in the form of a chart. Either a bar chart or a pie chart would be suitable, but as we will be showing percentages making up parts of a whole, a pie chart is particularly appropriate.

Copying cells to a new worksheet

First we need to copy the summary data from the survey analysis to a new worksheet.

- Open **Survey Method1** created in the last chapter.

- Drag down through row headers 1 to 4 to select these rows.

- Hold down the **Ctrl** key while you drag through row headers 81 to 94 to select these cells too.

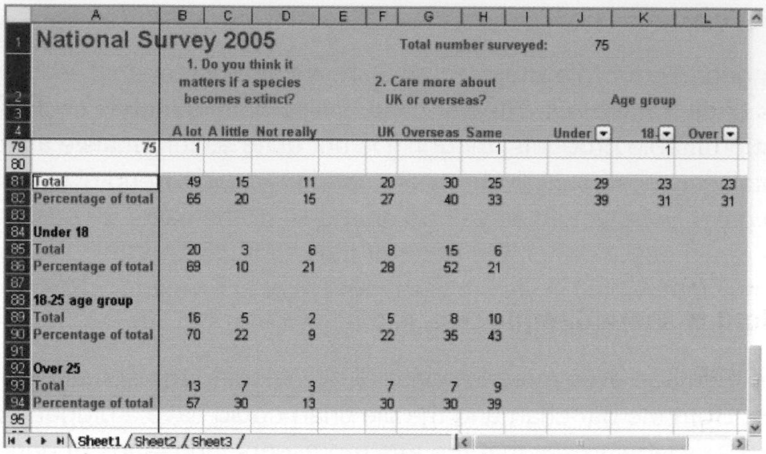

	A	B	C	D	E	F	G	H	I	J	K	L
1	National Survey 2005					Total number surveyed:				75		
2		1. Do you think it matters if a species becomes extinct?				2. Care more about UK or overseas?				Age group		
3												
4		A lot	A little	Not really		UK	Overseas	Same		Under	18-	Over
79	75	1						1			1	
80												
81	Total	49	15	11		20	30	25		29	23	23
82	Percentage of total	65	20	15		27	40	33		39	31	31
83												
84	Under 18											
85	Total	20	3	6		8	15	6				
86	Percentage of total	69	10	21		28	52	21				
87												
88	18-25 age group											
89	Total	16	5	2		5	8	10				
90	Percentage of total	70	22	9		22	35	43				
91												
92	Over 25											
93	Total	13	7	3		7	7	9				
94	Percentage of total	57	30	13		30	30	39				
95												

Sheet1 / Sheet2 / Sheet3

Figure 6.3

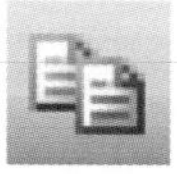

Copy

- Click the **Copy** button to copy these cells to the **Clipboard**.
- Click the **Sheet2** tab and, with the cursor in cell A1, select **Edit**, **Paste Special**.
- Select the **Values and Number Formats** option and click **OK**.
- Right-click the sheet tab for **Sheet2** and select **Rename**.
- Type the new name for this sheet, **Results**. Press **Enter**.
- Adjust column widths so that your sheet looks like Figure 6.4.

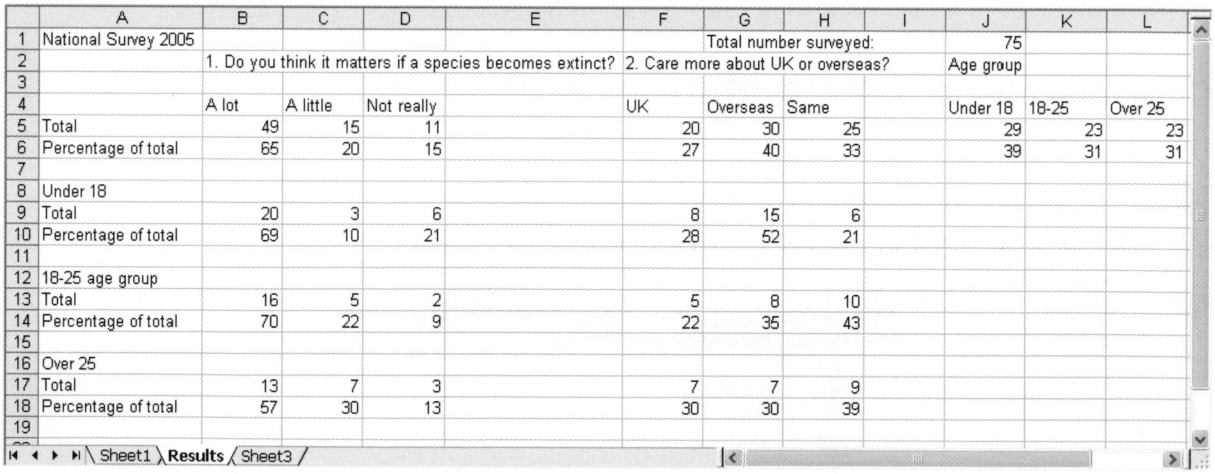

	A	B	C	D	E	F	G	H	I	J	K	L
1	National Survey 2005						Total number surveyed:			75		
2		1. Do you think it matters if a species becomes extinct?				2. Care more about UK or overseas?				Age group		
3												
4		A lot	A little	Not really		UK	Overseas	Same		Under 18	18-25	Over 25
5	Total	49	15	11		20	30	25		29	23	23
6	Percentage of total	65	20	15		27	40	33		39	31	31
7												
8	Under 18											
9	Total	20	3	6		8	15	6				
10	Percentage of total	69	10	21		28	52	21				
11												
12	18-25 age group											
13	Total	16	5	2		5	8	10				
14	Percentage of total	70	22	9		22	35	43				
15												
16	Over 25											
17	Total	13	7	3		7	7	9				
18	Percentage of total	57	30	13		30	30	39				
19												

Sheet1 / Results / Sheet3

Figure 6.4

Creating a pie chart

We will start by creating two pie charts from the results for Question 1. The first pie chart will show the results of everyone included in the survey; the second one will show, for comparison purposes, the results for the Under 18 age group. This will help us to answer a question such as "Do young people care *more* or *less* than the average, whether a species becomes extinct?"

 Select cells B4 to D4. Keep your finger on the **Ctrl** key while you select cells B6 to D6.

 Click the **Chart Wizard** button and select **Pie** in the **Step 1** dialogue box. You can use the **Press and Hold to View Sample** button to see what the chart will look like. Click **Next**.

 Click **Next** in **Step 2**.

 In **Step 3**, enter the title **Do you think it matters if a species becomes extinct?**

 Click the **Data Labels** tab and select **Category Name** and **Percentage**.

Chart Wizard

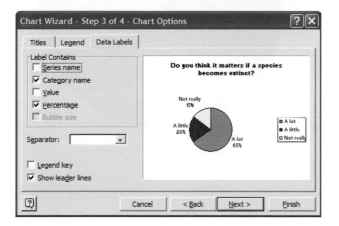

Figure 6.5

 Click the **Legend** tab and deselect **Show Legend**. Click **Next**.

 In **Step 4**, specify that you want to place the pie chart in a new sheet named **Pie Charts**, as in Figure 6.6.

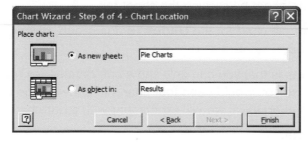

Figure 6.6

Click **Finish**. Your chart will appear as shown in Figure 6.7.

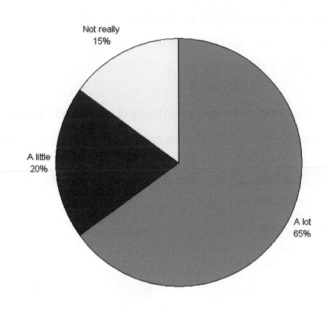

Do you think it matters if a species becomes extinct?

Not really
15%

A little
20%

A lot
65%

Figure 6.7

We can improve the chart by making the heading larger and adding a sub-heading to say that this chart refers to all respondents.

 Click in the chart title to select it. Now change the font size to **18** using the **Formatting** toolbar.

Click at the end of the text and press **Enter**. Then type **(All respondents)**.

Return to the **Results** sheet by clicking the sheet tab.

Now create a second pie chart for the **Under 18** age group, placing it in a new sheet named **Pie Chart1 Under 18**.

The problem with pie charts is that you can only show one data series (such as one particular age group) in each chart, so you would need four charts to show all the results we have collected just for Question 1. As an alternative, we will experiment with a bar chart.

Save your spreadsheet.

Creating a bar chart

Before we create the next chart we will copy the results data to another sheet, and then delete everything except the data that we want to chart.

 Click the **Results** worksheet tab, and hold down **Ctrl** while you drag it to the right. A little **+** sign will appear to show that the sheet will be copied instead of moved. Release the mouse button. The new sheet will be named **Results (2)**.

We will be making a bar chart of the responses to Question 2.

 Delete columns B, C, D and E by dragging across the column headers, right-clicking and selecting **Delete**.

 Delete rows 5, 9, 11, 13 and 17, which hold the total number of responses. We only need the percentages.

 Delete all the other cells that are not needed and move the headings for each group to the rows containing the percentages. Your spreadsheet should end up looking like this:

	A	B	C	D	E
1	National Survey 2005				
2		2. Care more about UK or overseas?			
3					
4		UK	Overseas	Same	
5	Total	27	40	33	
6	Under 18	28	52	21	
7	18-25 age group	22	35	43	
8	Over 25	30	30	39	
9					

Figure 6.8

 Select cells A4 to D8 and press the **Chart** button. This time, select **Column** as the type of chart. Press **Next**, and **Next** again.

 Look at all the options in **Step 3** of the **Chart Wizard**. Add a chart title, and a **Value (Y) axis**, calling it **Percentage**.

 Leave the chart in the current worksheet, **Results(2)**.

Your chart will look something like the one in Figure 6.9. You can move it by selecting the chart area and dragging the whole chart, or resize it by dragging one of the selection handles.

If you want to edit the axis labels, for example to change **18-25 age group** to **18-25**, just edit the text in the original cell (in this case, A7).

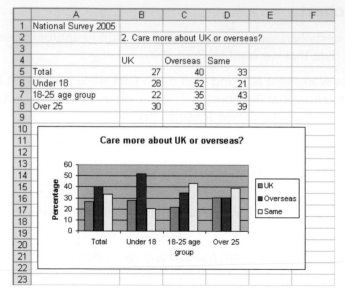

Figure 6.9

Adding a header and footer

It is always a good idea to insert a header and footer on your worksheets, to give important information such as the worksheet name, your own name and the creation date.

 Make sure the chart is not selected, then from the main menu select **View**, **Header and Footer.**

 Click the **Custom Header** button and select the options shown in Figure 6.10 by clicking the appropriate icons.

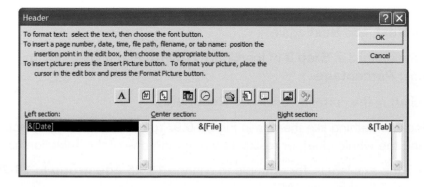

Figure 6.10

 Click **OK**.

 Insert a custom footer: you can type your own name in the left corner. Click **OK**.

The header and footer should appear like this in the **Page Setup** window:

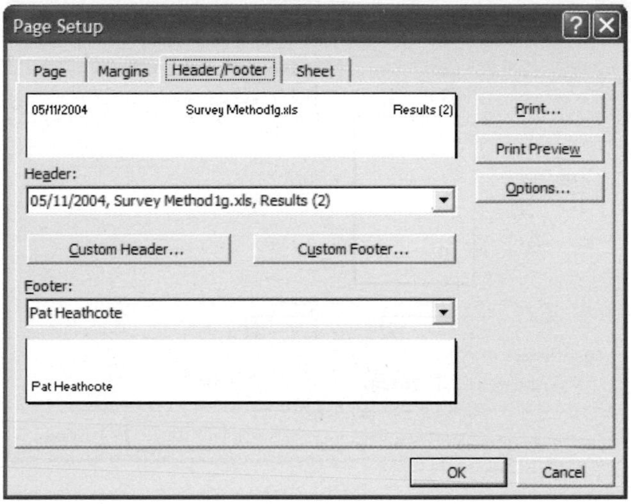

Page Setup dialog box:

Tabs: Page | Margins | Header/Footer | Sheet

Preview box: 05/11/2004   Survey Method1g.xls   Results (2)

Header:
05/11/2004, Survey Method1g.xls, Results (2)

Custom Header...   Custom Footer...

Footer:
Pat Heathcote

Pat Heathcote

Buttons: Print... Print Preview Options... OK Cancel

Figure 6.11

▶ Click **OK**.

Printing selected areas

▶ Click the **Print Preview** button to see what will be printed. The data and the graph will both be shown.

Print Preview

If you want to print just the figures, you can set the print area by selecting the cells to print and then clicking **File**, **Set Print Area** from the main menu.

If you want to print just the chart, select it before clicking the **Print Preview** button. You can return to the spreadsheet by clicking the **Close** button or by pressing **Esc**.

Centring the data on the page

You can centre both the data and the chart on the printed page.

▶ With the chart deselected, click the **Print Preview** button.

▶ Click the **Setup...** button.

▶ In the **Margins** tab select **Center on page**, **Horizontally**.

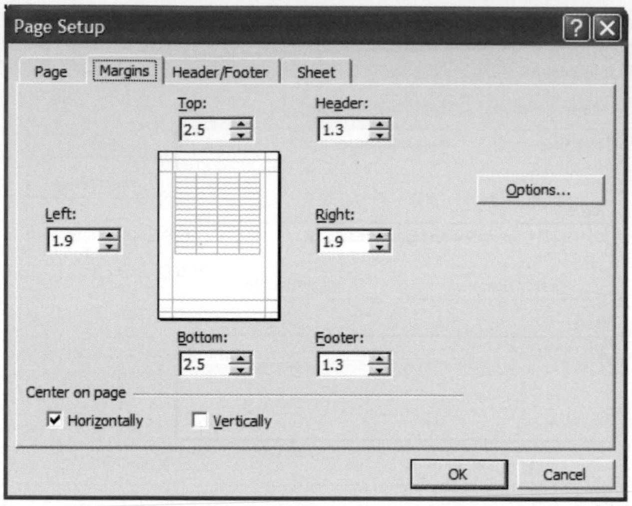

Figure 6.12

⊙ Click **OK**. Your page should appear as follows in **Print Preview**:

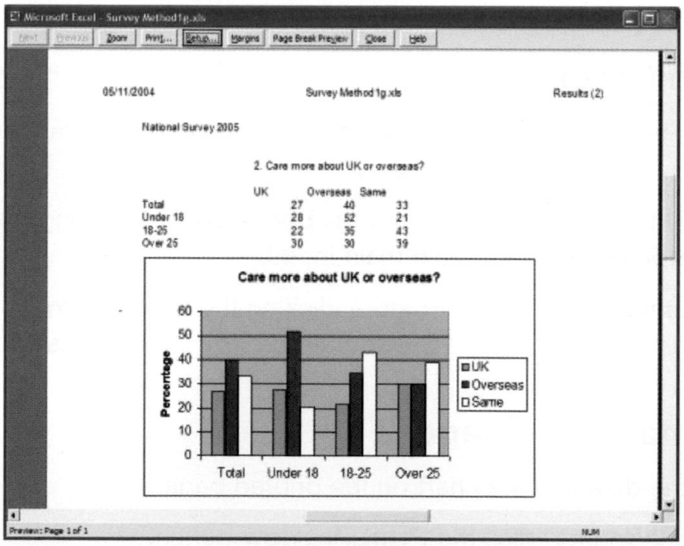

Figure 6.13

⊙ Save and close your spreadsheet.

In the next chapter we'll look at how you could show this data in a PowerPoint presentation.

Chapter 7 – Presenting Results

In this chapter we will develop a PowerPoint presentation which will be delivered to a group of marketing managers and staff at the headquarters of the charity that performed the survey we analysed in the last chapter.

Planning a presentation

To deliver an effective presentation you must consider who your audience is, and prepare your slides to suit them. Depending on the audience, you might use formal or informal language. You might use very simple language for a young audience or more complex language for a group of managers.

Whoever your presentation is for, here are a few basic guidelines.

- Start with a title screen showing what the presentation is about.
- Don't put more than four or five points on a slide. People can't concentrate on too much information at once.
- Keep each point short and simple. You can add more detail during delivery as you talk around the subject.
- Sound, graphics and animation can all add interest, but don't overdo them!

You will need to consider exactly what information you want to get across in your presentation. In this example, you could show:

- a title slide;
- the facts about the survey conducted, including its purpose, when and where it was carried out and how many people were surveyed.

For each question in the survey, you should include:

- the actual question;
- an analysis of the responses;
- a chart illustrating the result;
- a conclusion;
- recommended actions to be taken following the survey.

Starting PowerPoint

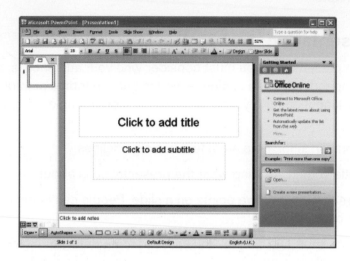 Load PowerPoint. Your screen will look like this:

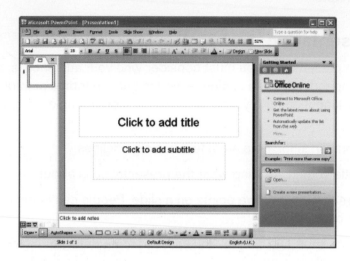

Figure 7.1

Using a template

A quick way to create a presentation with a consistent style and colour scheme is to use a template.

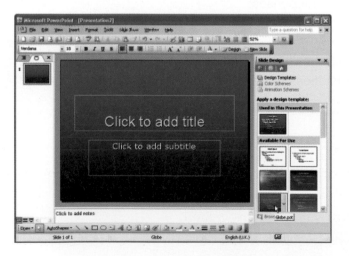 From the main menu select **File, New**.

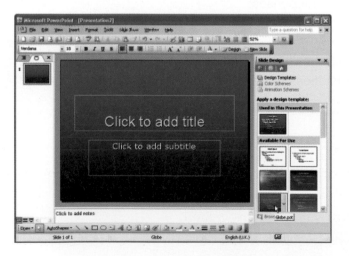 In the **New Presentation** task pane on the right of the screen, click **From Design Template**.

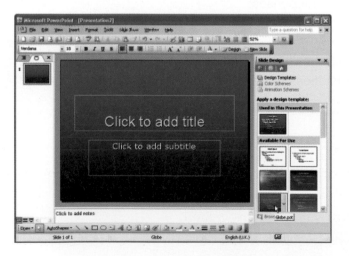 Select **Globe** or another suitable template. Your screen will look like Figure 7.2.

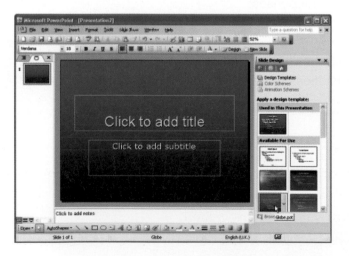

Figure 7.2

Adding text to the title screen

Each slide layout displays **placeholders** that allow you to add objects such as text, a clip art image or a chart.

 Click the **title** placeholder and type **Global Environment Association**.

 Click the **subtitle** placeholder and type **Results of National Survey 2005**.

Starting a new slide

 Click the **New Slide** button on the **Standard** toolbar.

New Slide

The third layout, **Title and Text**, is already selected for you by PowerPoint in the **Slide Layout** pane.

 Add the text as shown on the following screenshot.

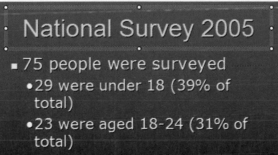

Figure 7.3

 Tip:

Use the **Increase Indent** and **Decrease Indent** buttons to get different levels of bullet. Then select a text box and click the **Increase Font Size** button several times until you are satisfied with the look of your slide.

Checking your spelling

You can check your spelling either by using a main menu command or by clicking the **Spelling and Grammar** button.

 Click the **Spelling and Grammar** button.

 If you have made any spelling errors, PowerPoint will find them for you.

Spelling and Grammar

Formatting your slides

The next four slides will show the four questions, and explain that the responses are analysed by age group.

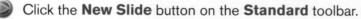 Click the **New Slide** button on the **Standard** toolbar.

Add text as shown in Figure 7.4.

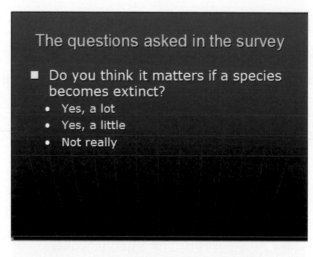

The questions asked in the survey

■ Do you think it matters if a species becomes extinct?
- Yes, a lot
- Yes, a little
- Not really

Figure 7.4

This slide can be improved a lot. You can change the first bullet point to a numbered point for Question 1, and you can make the round bullets look more like tick boxes.

Select the square bullet point, and then click the **Numbering** button. If you want the number smaller or bigger, select **Format, Bullets and Numbering** from the main menu.

Bullets and Numbering [?][X]

Bulleted | Numbered

| None | 1. ——— 2. ——— 3. ——— | 1) ——— 2) ——— 3) ——— | I. ——— II. ——— III. ——— |

| A. ——— B. ——— C. ——— | a) ——— b) ——— c) ——— | a. ——— b. ——— c. ——— | i. ——— ii. ——— iii. ——— |

Size: 100 % of text   Start at: 1

Color:

Reset   OK   Cancel

Figure 7.5

Now you can select the three bullet points for the responses and customise them.

 Select the bullet points and choose **Format**, **Bullets and Numbering** from the main menu.

 Select the bottom right bullet type (ticks) and then click **Customise**.

 Select the big square symbol, which should appear in the **Recently used symbols** list (if it doesn't, find it in the **Wingdings 2** font). Click **OK**.

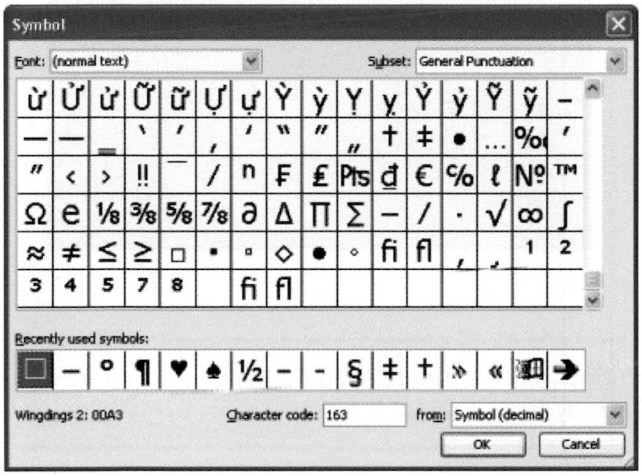

Figure 7.6

 In the next window, change the colour and size of the bullet if you want to, and click **OK**.

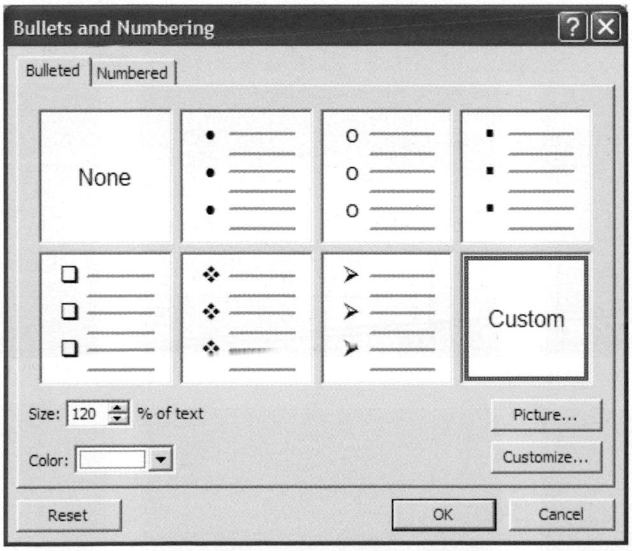

Figure 7.7

67

Now add text as shown in Figure 7.8.

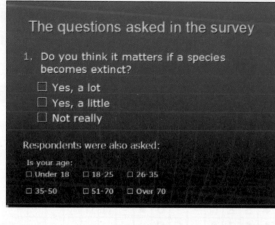

Figure 7.8

Tip:

You will need to use the **Bullets** and **Decrease Indents** buttons, the menu command **Insert Symbol** and the **Tab** key.

Moving slides

You can change the order of your slides if you need to. Just click the slide icon and drag it to where you want it.

 Now add slides for the other three questions.

 Look at your slides in **Slide Sorter** view. They will look something like this:

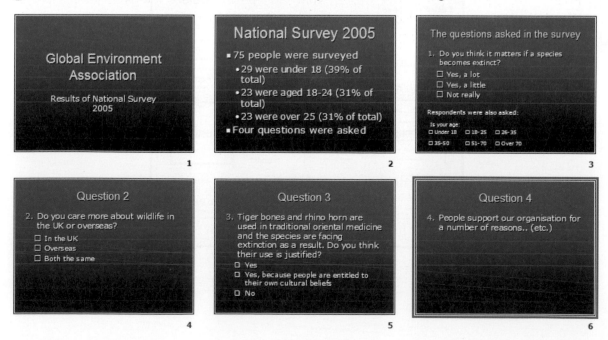

Figure 7.9

Saving different versions of your work

It is really important to be able to show the development of your work in the final eportfolio that you will present to the examiner. To do this you should rename the file you are working on each time you make substantial changes.

- Click **File** on the main menu and select **Save As**.

- Save this presentation now as **SurveyPresentation v1** in your **Survey Results** folder. The **v1** shows that this is version 1 of the presentation.

Next time you save, you should call it **SurveyPresentation v2**, and so on. This will show the examiner your sequence of development and show how you changed your ideas as you went along, before coming up with the final version. It is a bit like showing your workings in a maths exam. You will be awarded marks for showing these versions.

Presenting the analysis

The next stage is to present the results of the analysis. This is probably best done by showing charts similar to the ones we created in Excel.

- In **Normal** view, insert a new slide and change the layout to **Title and Content** (the third layout under **Content Layouts**).

- Add a heading, **Question 1 results**.

- Click the **Insert Chart** icon on the **Standard** toolbar.

Insert Chart

- You will then see a small spreadsheet like you would see in Excel. Notice that some of the icons on the **Standard** toolbar have changed.

- Fill in the results from the questionnaire. What you type will replace the placeholders **East**, **West**, **North**, and so on, which were inserted by default.

- Right-click in the column header above **4th Qtr** and delete this column.

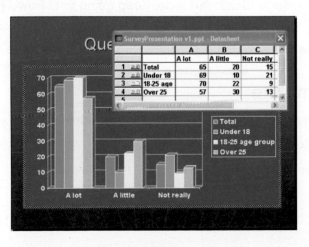

Figure 7.10

69

While editing the chart, you can hide or show the datasheet by selecting **View**, **Datasheet** from the main menu.

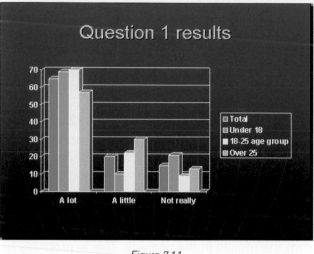

Figure 7.11

 Insert three more slides with the same format for questions 2, 3 and 4. Add headings to each slide – you can complete these slides later.

 Add a final slide with a **Title and Text** layout, and give it the heading **Conclusion**.

Viewing a slide show

You can view your slide show to see what it looks like, and where it needs a little brightening up.

 In **Slide Sorter** view, click the first slide.

 Click the **Slide Show** button beside the **Slide Sorter** view button in the bottom left of the window.

 Click the mouse to change to the next slide. Keep going until PowerPoint returns you to **Slide Sorter** view, or press **Esc** at any time.

 Click **File**, **Save As** and save the presentation again as **SurveyPresentation v2**.

Changing the template

You can experiment with different templates even after you have created your slides.

 Select **Format**, **Slide Design** from the menu.

 Choose another template – the one in Figure 7.12 is **Fireworks**.

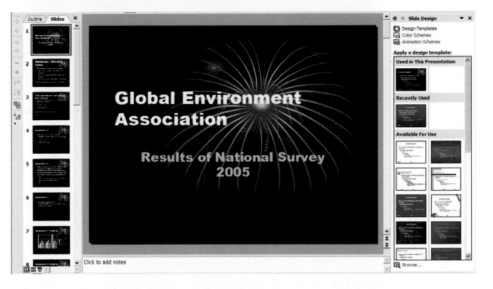

Figure 7.12

As this is a completely inappropriate template for the subject matter, we will revert to the original template.

Undo

 Click the **Undo** button on the **Standard** toolbar.

There are other ways of changing the appearance of your slides. We will try a different colour scheme.

Changing the slide colour scheme

 With any slide selected, select the **Colour Schemes** option at the top of the **Slide Design** pane.

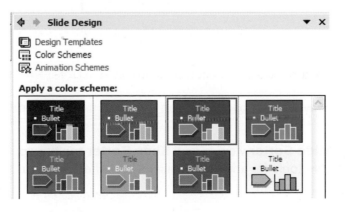

Figure 7.13

The green one isn't bad! Take your pick.

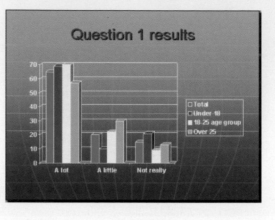

Figure 7.14

Note that you can also change the background styles and colours of any or all slides.

- Select the slides you want to change, and choose **Format**, **Background** from the menu bar.

- Click the small down-arrow in the **Background fill** box and select a colour.

Figure 7.15

Transitions

Transitions change the way a slide opens. You can make the next slide open like a blind or curtain, for example.

You will notice that, in **Slide Sorter** view, a new **Slide Sorter** toolbar appears somewhere on the screen. This has all the tools for adding transitions and effects to your slides.

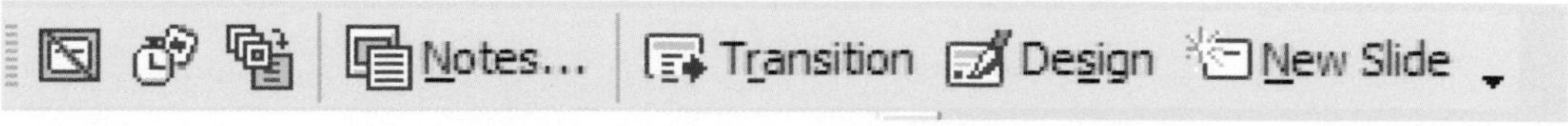

Figure 7.16

With **Slide 1** selected, click the **Transition** button on the toolbar.

A **Slide Transition** pane opens:

Figure 7.17

Scroll down the list of transitions and select **Fade Through Black**. This will make the first screen fade in from a black background.

Click **Apply to All Slides**. You can try out the effect by clicking the **Slide Show** button in this window.

You can try out other effects, such as adding sounds, from this window.

You will notice that a small icon appears underneath each slide in **Slide Sorter** view. This represents a transition action.

Transition action

You can experiment with other special effects by selecting **Slide Show, Animation Schemes** from the menu.

Inserting graphics and clip art

You can insert pictures to brighten up your presentation. We will insert two graphics into **Slide 4**: one clip art picture and one picture stored as a file. You can download **tiger.jpg** from the website **www.payne-gallway.co.uk/didaD201.**

In **Normal** view, click **Slide 4**. Click below the text and from the menu select **Insert, Picture, Clip Art.**

In the **Clip Art** task pane, type **badger** in the **Search for** box. Click the picture of the badger to insert it.

The badger will be inserted, but it is too big.

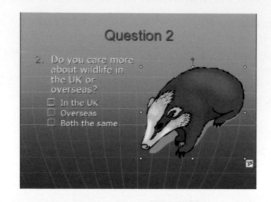

Figure 7.18

▶ Drag a corner handle inwards to make the graphic smaller. Then drag the whole graphic underneath the text. You could also resize the text box – experiment!

▶ Click away from the graphic to deselect it.

▶ From the menu select **Insert**, **Picture**, **From File** and find the file **tiger.jpg**.

▶ Resize and move the picture of the tiger so that the slide looks like Figure 7.19.

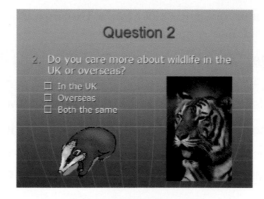

Figure 7.19

▶ Save the presentation as **SurveyPresentation v3**.

Questions:

Do you like the final effect? Do you think that mixing clip art and photographic images on the same slide works well? What is the purpose of inserting these images?

Think very carefully, when you create your own presentations, about the overall design and how best to use graphic images. Don't use an image just because you happen to have one handy, or because you want to show you know how to do this.

Inserting a chart from a spreadsheet

Earlier on, we created a chart from scratch in PowerPoint. If you already have one in a spreadsheet, you can copy and paste it into PowerPoint. You will find you need to increase the size of the labels before copying, so that they are big enough to be clearly seen in a presentation.

- Go to your saved spreadsheet **Survey Method1.xls**, and select the **Results(2)** worksheet. Right-click the chart area and select **Copy**.

- In your presentation, in **Normal** view, display **Slide 8**: **Question 2 results**.

- Right-click the content area, and select **Paste**. The chart will be inserted, as shown in Figure 7.20.

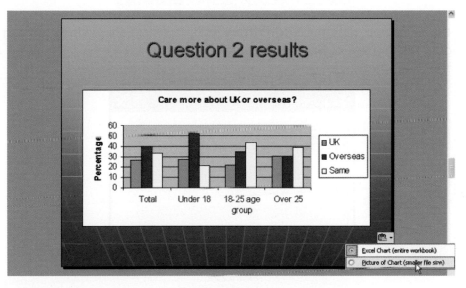

Figure 7.20

- Click the **smart tag** which appears, and select **Picture of Chart (smaller file size)**.

- Resize the resulting picture.

Speaker notes

The best presentation in the world is of little use if the person delivering it is ill-prepared or a poor presenter. Remember that the presentation is not designed to run on its own – you will have to stand up and deliver it to an audience, talking about each slide as you show it. You will need to rehearse this, and make sure that the transitions and special effects don't become tedious, that any sounds you have added are not merely irritating, and that the text is clearly legible from the back of the room.

To help you remember what you need to say, you can produce speaker notes. These will be visible on your computer but will not appear on the screen.

 Select **Slide 3**. We will add some notes as a reminder of what to say while the slide is on the screen.

 At the bottom of the screen there is a box saying **Click to add notes**. Type the text shown in Figure 7.21 into this box.

> Respondents were also asked to tick a box specifying Male or Female. This was not used in the final analysis of results.

Figure 7.21

 With **Slide 3** selected, click the **Slide Show** icon. The slide show starts running from that point. Right-click and select **Screen**, **Speaker Notes** from the menu. The notes appear on your screen.

Figure 7.22

 Press **Esc** twice, to close this dialogue and to exit from the slide show.

Printing your slides

You can print out your slides, several to a page, to hand out to the audience after the presentation.

 From the menu select **File**, **Print**.

 Select **Handouts** from the **Print What** option box, as shown in Figure 7.23.

 Choose your preferred number of **Slides per page** and click **OK**.

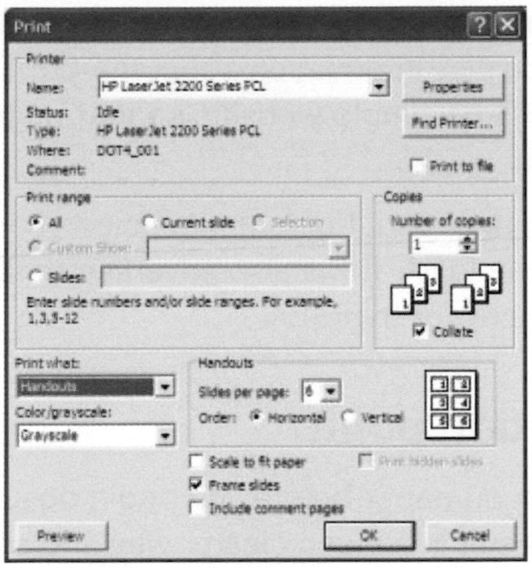

Figure 7.23

Save your presentation as **SurveyPresentation v4**.

You now have the skills to fill in the other slides to complete this presentation! Remember to continue saving different versions.

Good marks... ✓

You will get good marks for your presentation if you:

- are consistent throughout the presentation – use the same fonts, colour scheme and background for every slide;
- make sure your images are relevant and of good quality;
- pay attention to the design of each slide and position every object sensibly, in a suitable size (be careful not to distort graphics when resizing them);
- don't put too much information onto one slide;
- spell check and proofread every slide carefully;
- acknowledge copyright for images used.

Bad marks... ✗

You will lose marks for your presentation if you:

- do not take into account your target audience;
- use WordArt or clip art inappropriately;
- use irrelevant images or text;
- have spelling or grammar mistakes in your presentation;
- use other people's work without acknowledging them;
- create a presentation which is the same as someone else's.

For Task 9, you need to create an interactive information point. This information point is for teenagers at a school, and will display information about the GEA. It will run completely automatically, in a similar manner to a simple website, so that visitors can select just the information they are interested in.

The presentation will give information about different species of animal around the world, and list ways in which people can help the GEA. It will also advertise details of a concert that the school is putting on in order to raise money for the GEA.

Planning your information point

You should plan the presentation on paper before you begin designing it on the computer. This way you can envisage the end result in a much clearer way and see exactly what you will need to do. This will also help you to estimate how long it will take to create, so you can make any adjustments to your overall project plan.

You will use PowerPoint for the information point. Below is a rough plan for each of the slides. In it there is a map with links to several different animals, an animal noise game and some other slides with information about the concert. You can also plan how the slides will link to each other.

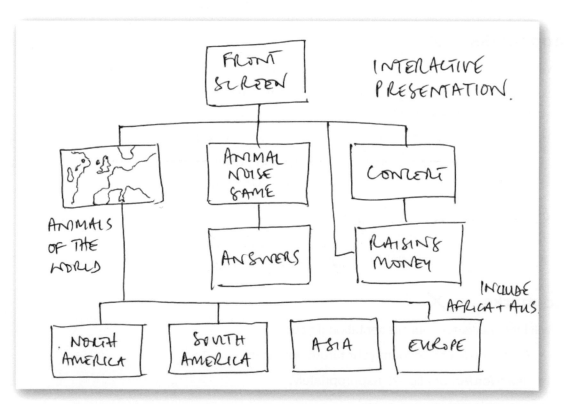

Figure 8.1: The plan

Setting up the presentation

At this stage, you will decide on a rough colour scheme and add all the slides into the presentation as blanks, each with just a title.

 Open PowerPoint to create a new blank presentation.

 With the **Slide Layout** task pane on display, select **Title Only** from the **Text Layouts** section.

 Click the title placeholder and type **Welcome to the GEA**.

Figure 8.2: Selecting a layout

 Close the **Slide Layout** task pane.

 Right-click the slide and select **Background** from the pop-up menu.

 Click the down-arrow and select **More Colors** from the list of options.

Choose a **Pale Blue** and click **OK**.

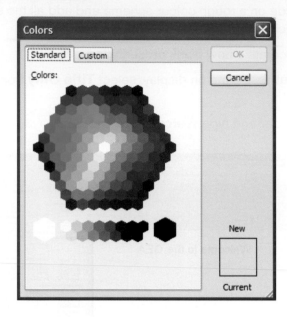

Figure 8.3: Choosing a background colour

 Now click **Apply to All**. This will cause all future slides to share the same background.

It is important to maintain a consistent appearance on each slide by using only a small selection of colours. You should make sure that you do the same thing with font styles and sizes.

Now you are going to add some more colour to build up the overall look of the presentation.

 Click **View**, **Toolbars** and make sure that **Drawing** is selected.

Rectangle

 Click the **Rectangle** tool and draw out a shape as high as the slide but only a sixth as wide. Move it the far left of the screen.

 Double-click the shape to get the **Format AutoShape** window.

Format AutoShape

| Colors and Lines | Size | Position | Picture | Text Box | Web |

Fill

Color: [dark color dropdown]

Transparency: ◀ ▓ ▶   0 %

Line

Color: No Line   Style:

Dashed: Weight: 0.75 pt

Connector:

Arrows

Begin style: End style:

Begin size: End size:

☐ Default for new objects

[OK]   [Cancel]   [Preview]

Figure 8.4: Formatting an AutoShape

▶ Change the **Fill Color** to **Dark Blue** and the **Line Color** to **No Line**.

▶ Click **OK**.

▶ Place another (**Dark Green**) rectangle along the bottom of the screen. Position it like the one in Figure 8.5.

▶ Finally, add a line using the **Line** tool across the top of the dark green box.

▶ Make the line a solid **Lime** colour with a weight of **10pt**. This will add impact.

Line

Welcome to the GEA

Figure 8.5

▶ Make sure that the title is left-aligned and starts slightly to the right of the blue rectangle.

Duplicating slides

Now you need to copy this slide to ensure that all the others have the boxes in exactly the same place.

 With the slide selected in the **Slides** pane on the left of the screen, select **Edit, Duplicate** from the main menu.

 This will create another slide, identical to the first. As a shortcut, try pressing **Ctrl+D** on the keyboard. Repeat this until you have **12** slides.

 Save the presentation as **GEAInformationPoint.ppt** in the **GEA Presentation** folder.

Creating a title slide

It is a good idea, once you have created the overall design of your slides, to give your first slide a slightly different look for extra impact.

 Select the first slide in the **Slides** pane.

 Now rearrange the blocks of colour so that they look like those in Figure 8.6. You will need to delete the lime green line and replace it with a narrow rectangle. Don't worry about covering up the text. Add a long black rectangle down the edge of the blocks.

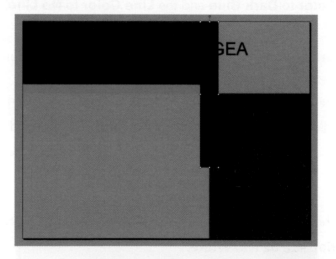

Figure 8.6: Designing a title screen

 Select **Insert, Picture, From File** from the menu and add the **RhinoAndBaby.jpg** file. You should already have this from Chapter 3; if not, you can download it from **http://www.payne-gallway.co.uk/didaD201** or find a similar one on the Internet.

▶ Right-click the image and select **Show Picture Toolbar** if it is not already visible.

▶ Click the **Set Transparent Color** tool and click the white area of the image.

▶ Now click the **Draw** button on the far left of the **Drawing** toolbar and select **Rotate or Flip**, **Flip Horizontal**.

Set Transparent Color

▶ Use the corner handles to enlarge the image, and then position it in the bottom right of the slide.

Figure 8.7

▶ Drag the text below the dark green box and increase its **Font Size** to **66**. Make the text **Dark Blue** to match the box behind the rhino.

▶ Make it **Bold** then click the **Align Left** button.

Bold   Align Left

▶ Add another text box underneath it to say **Global Environment Association**.

▶ Set the text to **Arial**, size **32** and **White**.

Figure 8.8: The title slide

Creating the map slide

The second slide will show a simplified map of the world. The idea is that people will be able to click on a continent to display some information about the endangered species of that area of the world.

 Change the heading of **Slide 2** to **Endangered animals around the world...**

 Make it size **48, Bold**.

  Colour it **White** and click the **Align Left** button.

Align Left

Changing the order of objects

To bring the title forward so that it is on top of the dark blue box, you need to change the order.

 Right-click on the border of the text box and select **Order**, **Bring to Front**. (Alternatively, you can find the **Order** option on the **Draw** menu of the **Drawing** toolbar.)

Figure 8.9: Bringing an object to the foreground

Awareness of space

- Insert the **world-map.jpg** image into the slide.

- Use the **Set Transparent Color** tool on the **Picture** toolbar to remove the white background.

- Enlarge the image using only the corner handles, which prevent the image from being stretched out of proportion. Position it at the bottom of the slide, as shown in Figure 8.10.

Set Transparent Color

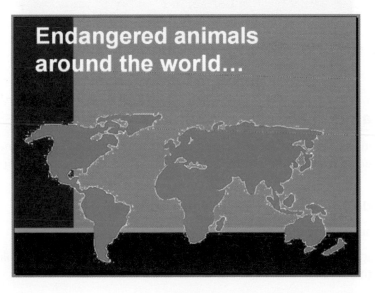

Figure 8.10

85

Because of the shape of the map, it will be better to rearrange the blocks of colour on the page. It is important to be aware of the space you leave around the objects on the page, as well as the objects themselves.

 Delete the green line and box from the bottom of the slide. (You might have to move the map out of the way to get at them.)

 Now resize the dark blue box to fill the area behind the map so it looks a little like a sea.

This divides up the page better, without it looking out of place in comparison with the other slides in the information point.

 Add a line of text below the title to say **Click on an area to see who lives where...**

 Make it **Arial 18** in **Black**.

 Use the same style of text to create labels for each of the areas on the map, as shown in Figure 8.11.

Figure 8.11: The map slide

Creating the animal slides

The next six slides in the presentation will be for the six areas marked on the map. Each slide will have two different animals from that particular area with a brief piece of information about each animal.

 Select the **Slide 3** and rename the title **North America**.

 Insert the image **BaldEagle.jpg**.

 Resize the image to make it smaller and position it overlapping the dark blue band in the top left under the title.

 Place the image **Bear.jpg** underneath the eagle.

▶ Resize the image so that it is exactly the same height as the eagle image. (This will be easier if you temporarily move the bear to the right of the eagle, so they touch.)

▶ Now use the **Crop** tool on the **Picture** toolbar to crop the bear image to match the width of the eagle.

Crop

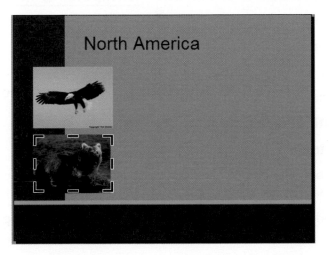

Figure 8.12: Cropping an image

> **Tip:**
>
> You should always try to make images identical sizes to improve the look and consistency of the presentation, but never try to stretch a photograph out of proportion.

Now you need to enter some text about each of creatures.

▶ Create two separate text boxes beside the images, as shown in Figure 8.13. The font should be **Black**, **Arial** size **18**.

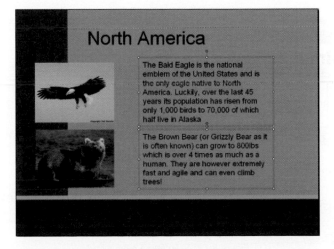

Figure 8.13: Adding text boxes

The next five slides are going to have the same format, but different text and images. The similarity of layout makes each slide look as though it 'belongs' to the presentation, and is not just a random add-on.

You can see screenshots of these slides in Figures 9.20a and 9.20b (pages 103–104). The images for the slides are available to download from **www.payne-gallway.co.uk/didaD201**.

▶ Add the slides in the following order:

      Slide 4 – **Europe**

      Slide 5 – **Asia**

      Slide 6 – **Africa**

      Slide 7 – **South America**

      Slide 8 – **Australia**

Slides 9 and 10 describe what people can do to help and include details of the concert that is being held to raise money for the GEA.

▶ Select **Slide 9** and change the title text to **What can you do to help?** Make it size **48** and **White**.

▶ Now resize the dark blue rectangle so it sits over the title text. Don't worry if the title seems to disappear!

▶ Right-click the dark blue rectangle and select **Order**, **Send to Back**. This will put it behind the text.

Changing the slide layout

This slide will have plenty of text so it would be a good idea to change the layout of the slide.

▶ Click **Format**, **Slide Layout** and select the **Title and Text** layout.

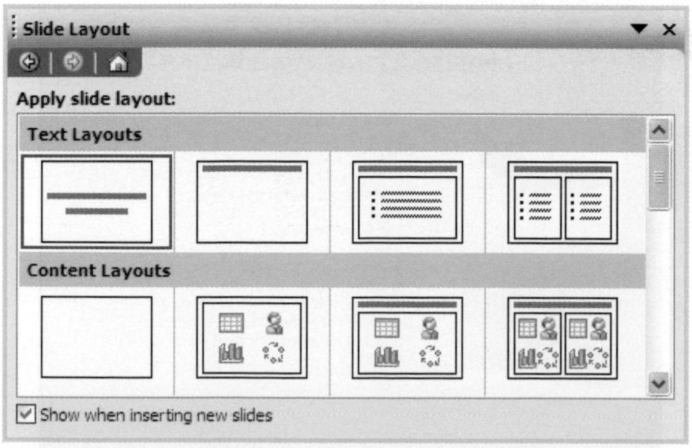

Figure 8.14: Selecting a new layout

Close the **Slide Layout** task pane.

 Enter the text shown in Figure 8.15. Make the sub-headings size **32** and the sub-text size **20**.

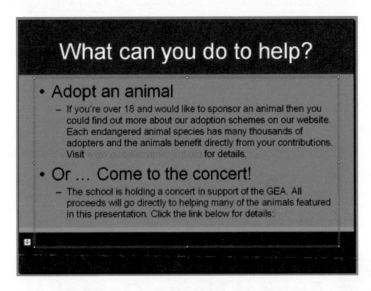

Figure 8.15

 Copy Figure 8.16 to complete Slide 10 in a similar way. The font size used here is **28**, and the title is size **60** in **Bold**.

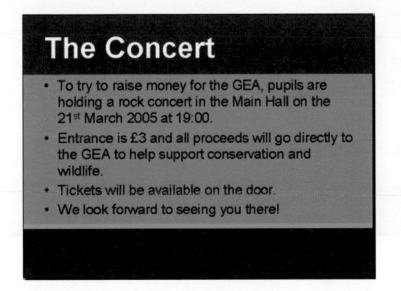

Figure 8.16: Slide 10

 Save the presentation.

In the next chapter you will finish off the presentation with buttons, hyperlinks, animation and sound! Every time you make a major change, use a new filename.

The information point you created in Chapter 8 is nearly finished, but you need to make it interactive so that the user can view whatever they are interested in. They need to feel in charge and be able to make the decision about what they see. To achieve this you will add buttons and hyperlinks. You will also add some animations and sounds to try to keep the attention of the current user and to gain the attention of other passers-by.

Firstly you need to finish off the presentation by adding in the final two slides. These will be an animal noise game!

Designing the slide

Since this part of the interactive presentation is slightly different from the rest, you can make it look slightly different too. Remember that it is still part of the whole presentation, so you can't make it look too dissimilar!

- In Slide 11, insert the title **Animal Noise Game!** Make it **Bold**, size **44**.
- Delete the two green bars from the bottom of the slide.

Figure 9.1: Animal noise game

Adding action buttons to play a sound

The idea of this game is that users can click on one of three buttons, which will each play a sound, and then guess which animal made the noise. For this part you will need to have downloaded the sounds from **www.payne-gallway.co.uk/didaD201**.

Warning:

You must take care when adding sounds to a PowerPoint presentation: although small sound files are embedded into the **.ppt** file, larger ones are only inserted as links to the sound file on disk. This minimises the size of the **.ppt** file, but makes it difficult to move the presentation between PCs.

The sound files we will be using go up to 259K, so we need to ensure that PowerPoint will still embed files of this size.

▶ From the main menu, select **Tools**, **Options**.

▶ On the **General** tab, set **Link sounds with file size greater than** to at least **300K**.

Now you can create the buttons for the sounds.

▶ From the main menu, select **Slide Show**, **Action Buttons** and select the **Custom** button.

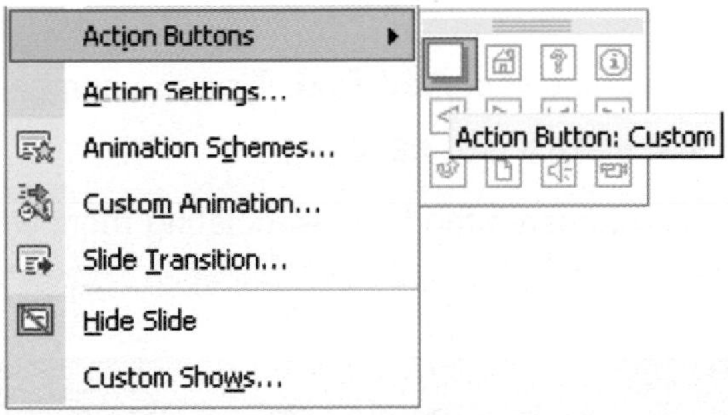

Figure 9.2: Adding an Action Button

▶ Drag out a square underneath the word 'Animal' in the title. Hold down the **Shift** key to get a perfect square.

▶ In the **Action Settings** window, select **Play Sound**.

▶ Scroll down to the bottom of the list of sounds and select **Other Sound**.

▶ Find the **Elephant.wav** sound file on your computer.

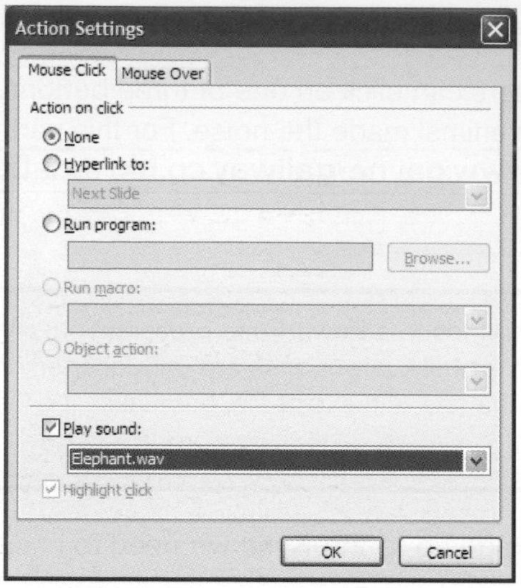

Action Settings

Mouse Click | Mouse Over

Action on click

○ None
○ Hyperlink to:
   Next Slide
○ Run program:
   [   ] Browse...
○ Run macro:
○ Object action:

☑ Play sound:
   Elephant.wav
☑ Highlight click

[OK] [Cancel]

Figure 9.3

- Click **OK**.

- Right-click on the button and select **Format AutoShape**.

- Change the **Fill Color** to **Dark Blue** to match the block on the left of the slide.

- Click **OK**.

- Right-click the button again and select **Add Text**. Type the number **1** into the button.

- Highlight the number **1** and make it size **66**, **Bold**.

- Create two more buttons underneath the first, associating them with **Lion.wav** and **Whale.wav** respectively.

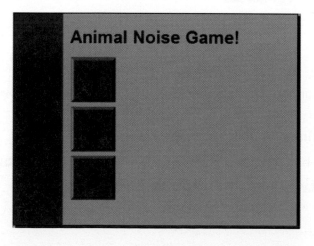

Figure 9.4

Click the **Slide Show** button in the bottom left of the screen, or press **Shift+F5** as a shortcut.

Test out your buttons!

If you aren't using speakers at your computer, you could try listening to the sounds on some headphones.

Now add some help text for the user, and a picture of a giraffe to brighten up the page. It is fine to hang the giraffe's neck off the edge of the page in order to fit it in, as shown in Figure 9.5.

Figure 9.5

Preventing objects from jumping

If you have the same object on more than one slide it is always best to use the copy and paste function rather than recreating it. This will automatically paste it in exactly the same position on the new slide.

Select the buttons on Slide 11 and click **Copy**.

Change to Slide 12 and click **Paste**. The buttons should appear in exactly the same positions as they did in Slide 11. This means that when someone skips between the slides in slide show view the buttons won't seem to jump.

Add the other slide elements shown in Figure 9.6.

View the show and try the difference for yourself.

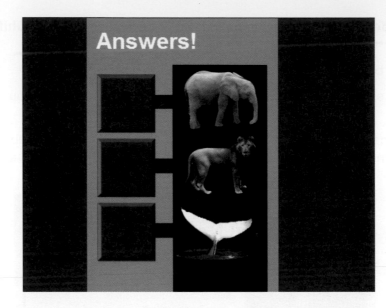

Figure 9.6

Adding navigation buttons

Navigation buttons are added in exactly the same way as the ones for the sounds; the difference is the action settings you apply to them.

 Select **Slide 11**.

 Choose **Slide Show**, **Action Buttons** from the menu, and click the **Custom** button. Drag out a small rectangular button in the bottom right of the slide.

 The **Action Settings** window will appear. In the **Hyperlink to** box select **Slide**.

Figure 9.7

⊚ Now select **12. Answers!** from the list of slides.

Figure 9.8: Inserting a hyperlink to another slide

⊚ Click **OK** and **OK** again.

⊚ **Format** the button to have a **Dark Green** background and **White** text, with the label **Answers**. You could also add a **Lime Green AutoShape** behind it to fill up some of the empty space and add impact.

Figure 9.9: Filling empty space with a block of colour

Now you can add a 'Back' button to the Answers slide. Ideally this should be formatted in the same way and be in the same place, so you can use the **Copy** and **Paste** functions to do this.

⊚ Select the **Answers** button and the lime green shape, and click **Copy**.

Copy

Paste

▶ **Paste** the button onto the **Answers!** slide.

▶ Right-click the new **Answers** button on **Slide 12**, and select **Action Settings**. Select the **Animal Noise Game!** slide from the **Action Settings** window and click **OK**.

▶ Edit the button text to say **Back**.

▶ Press **Shift+F5** to test the buttons. Do the buttons or the green box jump about or are they in the same positions on both slides? Press **Esc** to exit the show.

Adding 'Home' buttons

It is usually a good idea to have a button that will take the viewer back to the first slide. Often the person before may not reset the presentation back to the start, and you may want to look at it all from the beginning.

▶ Insert an **Action Button** in the bottom left of the **Answers!** slide.

▶ Hyperlink it to the first slide.

▶ Format it as shown in Figure 9.10 and add the **Home** text.

Figure 9.10

▶ When you are happy with it, copy the button and paste it onto every other slide except the first. The hyperlink properties will also be the same.

▶ Add more buttons onto the **North America** slide, as shown in Figure 9.11, and copy them to the other animal slides (4 to 8). The **Help the GEA** button should go to the **What can you do to help?** slide and the **Back to Map** button to the **Endangered Animals around the world** slide.

96

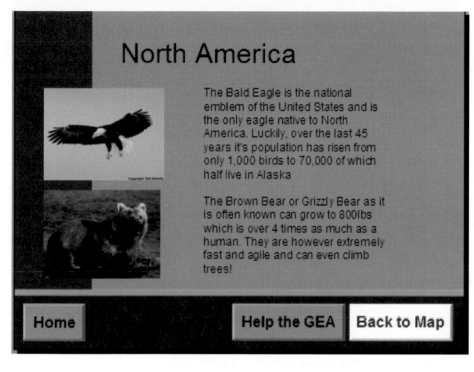

Figure 9.11

Add a **Concert Details** button to **Slide 9** and a **Back** button to **Slide 10**. Use the hyperlink plan in Figure 8.1 (page 78) or the finished slide in Figures 9.20a and 9.20b (pages 103–104) to help.

Save your presentation so far.

Adding a hotspot

A hotspot is an invisible button or AutoShape that has an action setting applied to it.

Click on the first slide.

Add the text shown in Figure 9.12. Adjust its size to fit the page, and make it **Yellow**.

Figure 9.12: Slide 1

You are going to make the entire slide a hyperlink to the next slide, apart from one area (the rhino), which will be linked to the game slide.

- Drag out a rectangle the size of the entire slide. It should cover everything.
- Right-click the new rectangle and select **Action Settings**.
- Select **Next Slide** from the **Hyperlink to** box and click **OK**.

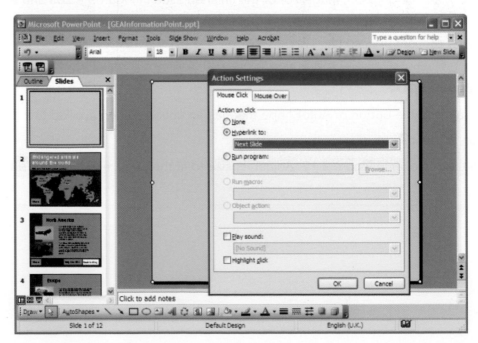

Figure 9.13

- Now right-click the rectangle and select **Format AutoShape**.

- Change the **Fill Color** to **No Fill** and the **Line Color** to **No Line**.

- Click the **Preview** button to make sure you can't see the rectangle any more, and click **OK**.

- From the **AutoShapes** menu on the **Drawing** toolbar, select a **Parallelogram** from the **Basic Shapes** options.

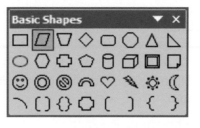

Figure 9.14

- Draw a rhino-size parallelogram over the top of the adult rhino.

- Right-click the shape and select **Format AutoShape**. Set the **Fill Transparency** to **60%** and click **OK**. This will help you adjust the size of the shape initially.

- Use the green **Rotate** handle to help position it as best you can over the animal.

Figure 9.15: Adding a hotspot

Set the **Action Setting** of the new shape to go to the **Animal Noise Game**.

 Format the **AutoShape** again to remove the fill and line completely.

Warning:

If an AutoShape has no fill colour then you can't select it by clicking inside it – you have to click its outline. Since the outline of the parallelogram is also hidden, selecting the shape if you need to change it is rather difficult!

 Test both the new hotspots. Note that the parallelogram will only work because it is on top of the larger rectangular hotspot.

 Select **Slide 2** and add more hotspots, in exactly the same way, to link to each of the animal slides around the world (see Figure 9.16).

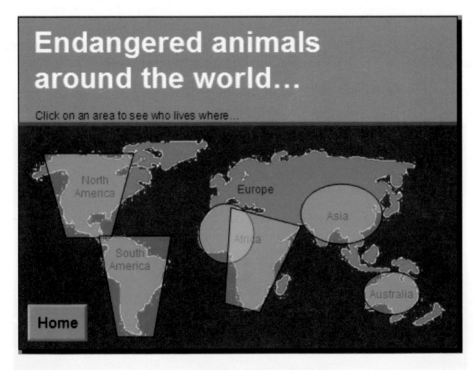

Figure 9.16: Adding hotspots to the map

Adding animation

You can animate objects on the slides to add more interest, but it is very easy to get carried away and make the show look a complete mess of gimmicks thrown together without much thought. It is best to select just one or perhaps two styles of animation and apply them to only a few objects.

 Select the **Animal Noise Game** slide.

 Click on the **Giraffe** and choose **Slide Show, Custom Animation** from the main menu.

Click the **Add Effect** button, then choose **Entrance**, **More Effects** and then click **Rise Up** from the **Moderate** selection of effects. Click **OK**.

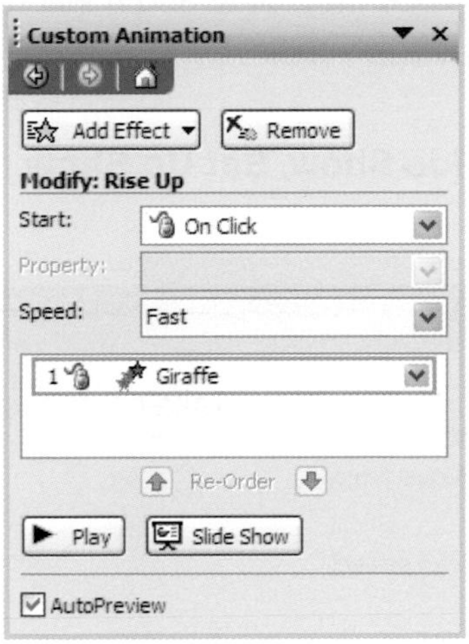

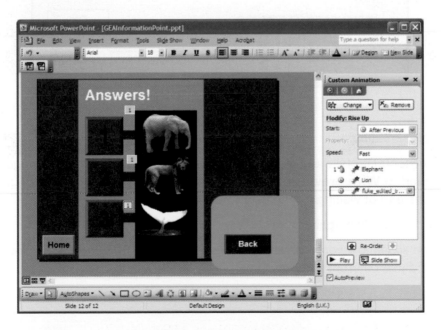

Figure 9.17: Adding animation to an object

Click the **Play** button to test the animation.

Change to the **Answers** slide and select the elephant.

Click **Add Effect**, **Entrance** and select the **Rise Up** effect again. Select the lion and the whale tail and do the same.

Figure 9.18: Animating multiple objects

Preview your animations in **Slide Show** view! Make sure that the elephant's black background has been set as the transparent colour.

Setting up the show

Unless you tell PowerPoint that this is intended to be a kiosk style presentation, when you run the show you will able to click anywhere on a slide and it will take you to the next automatically, regardless of what buttons or hotspots you have made. You may have noticed this when testing it yourself.

▶ From the main menu select **Slide Show**, **Set Up Show**. Set the **Show type** to **Browsed at a kiosk** and click **OK**.

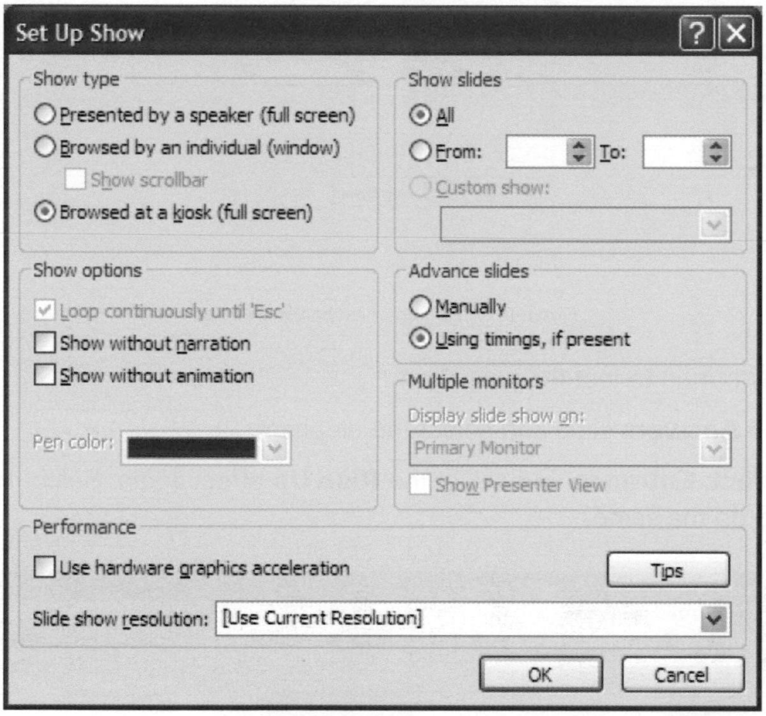

Figure 9.19: Setting up the show to run as an interactive kiosk

▶ **Save** the presentation.

▶ Test your presentation fully and make any corrections. You might like to change the giraffe's animation start to **With previous** so that the animation starts as soon as the slide is displayed, instead of waiting for the user to click.

▶ **Save** your presentation again.

You can finish the slideshow yourself with the help of Figures 9.20a and 9.20b. You can make up your own text, and use different pictures if you like.

The finished presentation

Here are the finished slides of the presentation:

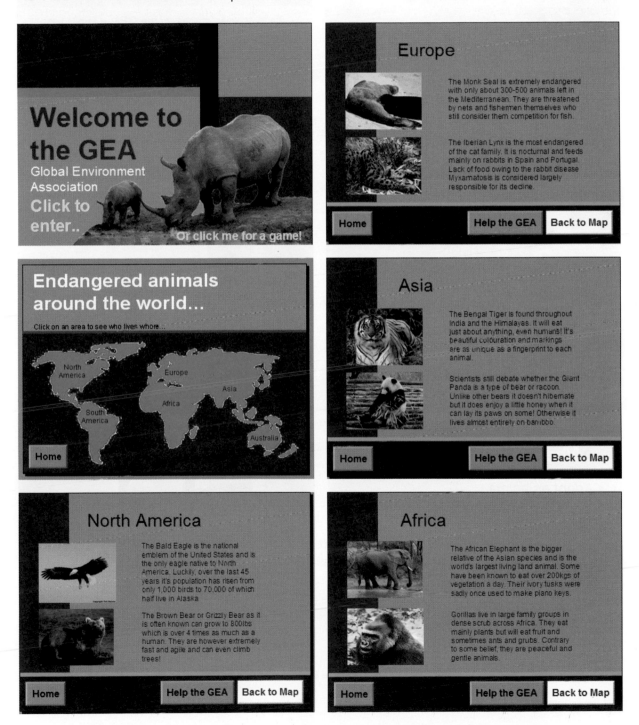

Figure 9.20a

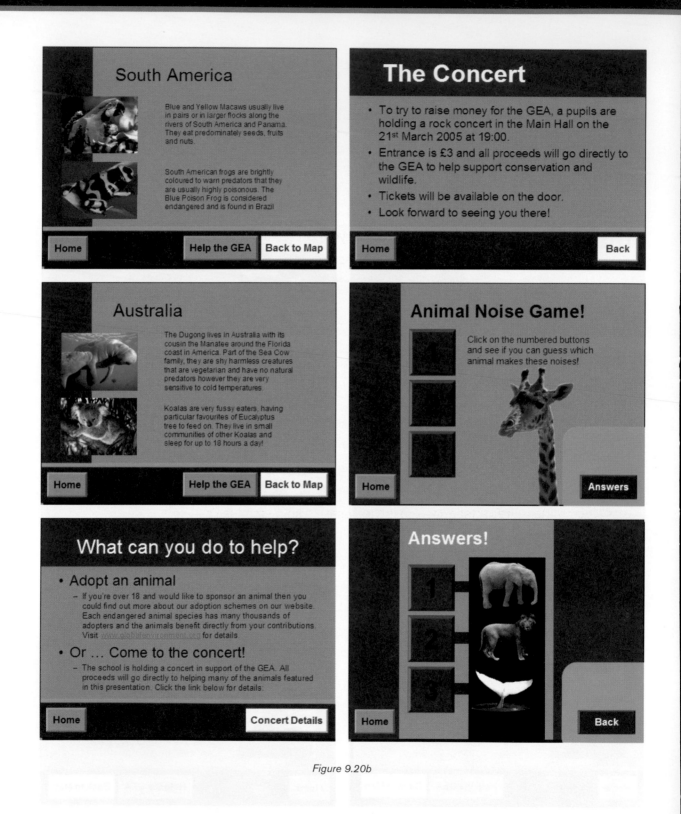

Figure 9.20b

Good marks... ✓

To get good marks for your presentation:

- make sure it is suitable for the target audience;
- make sure that it is easy to navigate around the presentation;
- make sure all the links work correctly;
- spell check and proofread every slide carefully;
- acknowledge copyright for images used;
- ask others for their feedback and modify your presentation to take it into account;
- show evidence of how the presentation developed;
- use your plan.

Bad marks... ✗

You will lose marks for your presentation if:

- the presentation has no interactivity;
- links do not work;
- you use WordArt, clip art, sound or transitions inappropriately;
- you have spelling or grammar mistakes in your presentation;
- you use other people's work without acknowledging them;
- you create a presentation which is the same as someone else's.

Chapter 10 – Creating a Database

The charity GEA has a database of donors who have responded to an appeal for funds, either by giving a one-off sum or by committing themselves to a monthly, quarterly or annual subscription. Everyone in the database has agreed that the charity may contact them by email in the future. From time to time, the charity may want to contact people in the database:

- to tell them about GEA's projects;
- to invite them to special events such as talks, exhibitions or fundraising events;
- to ask them if they would be prepared to increase their subscription.

The data items that have been collected for each donor are shown below.

1   DonorID
2   Title
3   Initial
4   Surname
5   Email address
6   Postcode
7   Telephone
8   Whether it is OK to telephone between 9 a.m. and 5 p.m. (Yes – Y, No – N)
9   Whether they wish their donations to go to a specific area (coded):
    UK – UK
    AF – Africa
    AS – Asia
    SA – South America
    XX – Any area
10 Whether they wish their donations to go towards saving a particular species (coded):
    TI – Tiger
    RH – Rhino
    OR – Orang-utan
    TU – Turtle
    GE – Golden Eagle
    XX – Any species
11 Date of last donation
12 Amount of donation
13 Monthly, quarterly, annual or occasional subscriber (coded):
    1 – Monthly
    2 – Quarterly
    3 – Annual
    4 – Occasional

Importing the data

The data is held in a text file called **GEADonors.csv** in the student resources section for this book, on the website **www.payne-gallway.co.uk/didaD201**. You will need to download this file and save it in a suitable folder.

Here is a small sample of the data:

```
1,Dr,K,Williamson,awilliamson9@aol.com,B16 8TR,0121 4645436,Y,XX,TI,30/06/2004,£25.00,1
2,Ms,P,Boyles,brinboyles@tiscali.co.uk,OL16 1SS,01706 291875,N,XX,XX,15/06/2004,£100.00,4
3,Mr,A,Henemulla,arizone@btinternet.com,NW10 8DY,0208 8383426,Y,XX,XX,15/07/2004,£40.00,3
4,Mr,B,Robinson,chris@seaford.ac.uk,NG34 7NY,01529 416195,Y,AF,TI,01/04/2004,£10.00,1
```

Data types

In this chapter you will be designing and creating the table for the database of donors. Before you start on this, you need to understand the different data types that may be used. The table below shows the main data types used in an Access database.

Data Type	Usage	Comments
Text	Alphanumeric data, i.e. any letter, number or other symbol that you can see on the keyboard	A field can be up to 255 characters.
Number	Numeric data	You can choose a whole number or a number with a decimal point. Each of these categories has several sub-categories in Access, depending on the size of the numbers you want to store – e.g. a whole number can be defined as **Byte** (0–255), **Integer** (−32,768 to 32,767) or **Long Integer** (for larger numbers).
Date/Time	Dates and times	For a date you should always use a **Date/Time** field, not a **Text** field, because Access can calculate with dates (e.g. find how many days between 03/09/2001 and 25/12/2001) but not with text.
Currency	Monetary data	
Yes/No	True/False data	Useful when a field can take only one of two possible values such as **Yes** or **No**, **True** or **False**.
AutoNumber	Often used for a key field – i.e. a field that uniquely identifies a record. No two records ever have the same key field.	This is a unique value generated by Access for each record.
Memo	Used for alphanumeric data	A **Memo** field can be up to 64,000 characters.

Figure 10.1: Data types

Designing the database table

A database table contains many **fields**, also called **attributes**.

When you design your own database, you should show a design for the table, which will show for each field:

Field name   This is what the field or attribute will be called. The fields have been given names **DonorID**, **Title**, **Initial**, **Surname**, etc.

It is best not to have spaces within field names, and, although they can be up to 64 characters, it is convenient to keep them brief but descriptive.

Data type   One of the types described in Figure 10.1.

Length   This applies to text fields, and shows how many characters there are in the field. It can be shown in brackets, as in Figure 10.2.

Validation rule   Validation rules are used to check that the data is allowable and sensible. Data that is not allowable or sensible should be rejected and an error message displayed. For example, **Sex** can only be **M** or **F**.

Description   Fields which are not self-explanatory may be given a short description to show what data the field will store. For example, **EmpNo** could be given the description **Unique Employee Number**.

Typical data   For each field, an example should be given of a typical value it might contain.

One field (or a combination of two or more fields) must be unique to each record in the database. This field is known as the **primary key**. For example, each record can be given a different Donor Identification Number (**DonorID**).

Question:

Why would it not be sensible to define the primary key of this database table as Surname, or even Surname + Initial?

Figure 10.2 shows the design for the **Donor** table.

Donor

Field name	Data type	Validation rule	Description	Typical data
DonorID	Auto Number	None – set by Access	Number used to identify a donor (Primary key)	7
Title	Text (6)	None – any value possible	Mr, Mrs, etc.	Mrs
Initial	Text (1)	Must be alphabetic	Donor's initial	G
Surname	Text (20)	None – any value possible	Surname of donor	Button
Email	Text (30)	None – any value possible	Email address of donor	ginabutton@hotmail.com
Postcode	Text (8)	None – any value possible	Postcode address of donor	IP12 4DC
Telephone	Text (15)	None – any value possible	Telephone number of donor	01473 244215
Daytime	Yes/No	Y or N	Whether it is OK to phone in daytime	Y
Area	Text (2)	UK, AF, AS, SA or XX	Code used to identify area to receive donation (XX = no restrictions)	XX
Species	Text (2)	TI, RH,OR, TU, GE or XX	Code used to identify species to receive donation. (XX = no restrictions)	TI
DateLast Donated	Date	Must be a valid date	Date of last donation	13/05/2001
Amount	Currency	Must be between £2 and £5,000	Amount of last donation	£50
Subscriber Type	Byte	1, 2, 3 or 4	Code used to identify whether monthly, quarterly, annual or occasional subscriber	4

Figure 10.2

Creating the database in Access

You're ready to create the database structure to hold the data!

 In the **Getting Started** task pane, select **Create a new file**, **Blank database** to open a new database.

A window opens asking you to choose a folder and a name for your new database.

 Select the **Database**, **GEA Donors** folder you have already created and name the database **GEADonors**. Access will automatically add the extension **.mdb**. Click **Create**.

The database window

Access databases are made up of objects. A **table** is an object, and is the only object we have talked about so far. Other objects, which you will come across in this book, include **queries**, **forms** and **reports**.

The **Database** window is a sort of central menu, from which you can open the objects in your database. The window has buttons for each type of database object (**Tables**, **Queries**, **Forms**, **Reports**, etc.).

Figure 10.3: The Database window

Tables is currently selected, and since at the moment there are no existing tables to **Open** or **Design**, only the **Create** options are active.

Creating a new table

▶ In the **Database** window, make sure the **Tables** tab is selected, and click **New**.

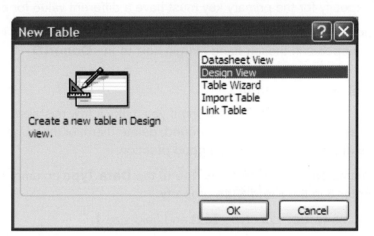

Figure 10.4: Creating a new table

▶ Select **Design View** and click **OK**.

The **Table Design** window appears.

Look back at the structure of the **Donor** table in Figure 10.2. All these fields need to be entered in the new table.

▶ Enter the first **Field Name**, **DonorID**, and tab to the **Data Type** column.

▶ Click the down-arrow and select **AutoNumber**.

▶ Tab to the **Description** column and type **Number used to identify a donor**.

Figure 10.5

Defining the primary key

Primary Key

Every table in an Access database should have a **primary key** (also known as the **key field**). The field which you specify for the primary key must have a different value for each record.

 With the cursor still in the row for the **DonorID**, press the **Primary Key** icon on the toolbar. The key symbol appears in the left-hand margin next to the **DonorID**.

Entering other fields

Now we can enter all the other fields. Don't worry if you make a few mistakes – after all the fields are entered you will learn how to move fields around, delete them, or insert new fields. You can correct any mistakes at that point, and it'll be good practice.

 Enter the field name **Title** in the next row. Tab to the **Data Type** column: the default is **Text**, which is fine. Enter **6** in the **Field Size** property.

 Enter the field name **Initial**, data type **Text** and field size **1**.

 Enter the other fields, giving them all the correct data type and length.

> **Tip:**
>
> Specify **2** decimal places for the **Amount** field. Be sure to give **SubscriberType** (the last field) the data type **Number**, and set its **Field Size** to **Byte**. Add an appropriate description wherever you think it is necessary.

Your table should look like this:

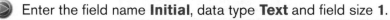

Figure 10.6: The Donor table

Saving the table structure

Save

▶ Save the table structure as **tblDonor** by pressing the **Save** button or selecting **File**, **Save** from the main menu. Don't worry if you have made some mistakes in the table structure – they can be corrected in a minute.

▶ Click the **Close** icon (**X**) in the top right-hand corner of the **Table Design** window to close it. You will be returned to the **Database** window.

Editing a table structure

In the **Database** window you will see that your new table is now listed.

Note:

If you have named the table wrongly, or made a spelling mistake, right-click the name and select **Rename**. Then type in the correct name. You cannot do this later, after you have created forms, queries or reports based on the table, without creating problems!

▶ Select the table name and click the **Design** button to return to **Design** view.

Design View

Inserting a field

To insert a new row for **Town** just above **Postcode**:

▶ Click the row selector (the left-hand margin) for **Postcode**.

▶ Press the **Insert** key on the keyboard or click the **Insert Rows** button.

▶ Enter the new field name, **Town**, data type **Text**.

Insert Rows

Deleting a field

To delete the field you have just inserted:

▶ Select the field by clicking in its row selector.

▶ Press the **Delete** key on the keyboard or click the **Delete Rows** button on the toolbar.

Delete Rows

Tip:

If you make a mistake, you can use **Edit**, **Undo Delete** to restore the field.

Moving a field

▶ Click the row selector to the left of the field's name to select the field.

▶ Click again and drag to where you want the field to be. You will see a line appear between fields as you drag over them to indicate where the field you are moving will be placed.

Primary Key

Changing or removing a key field

 To change the key field to **Surname**, click the row selector for the **Surname** field and then click the **Primary Key** button on the toolbar.

 To remove the primary key altogether, select the row that is currently the key field and click the **Primary Key** button on the toolbar.

 Sometimes a primary key is made up of more than one field (a **composite** or **compound** key). Select the first field (such as **Initial**), hold down **Ctrl** and select the second field (such as **Surname**). Then click the **Primary Key** button.

 When you have finished experimenting, restore **DonorID** as the primary key field of this table. Make any other necessary corrections to leave the fields as specified in Figure 10.6, and save the table structure.

Validation rules

Where possible, it is a good idea to enter **validation rules** to your table structure. This helps to ensure that the user does not accidentally enter wrong data.

We'll add some validation rules to fields in **tblDonor**.

 Click in the **Area** row and in the **Validation Rule** property, enter **UK or AF or AS or SA or XX**. Access will add quote marks automatically as soon as you move to a different property.

 Enter **Must be UK, AF, AS, SA or XX** in the **Validation Text** property, as shown in Figure 10.7.

Field Name	Data Type	Description
DonorID	AutoNumber	Number used to identify a donor
Title	Text	
Initial	Text	
Surname	Text	
Email	Text	
Postcode	Text	
Telephone	Text	
Daytime	Yes/No	Whether OK to phone in daytime
Area	Text	Donations to : UK, Africa, Asia, South America or no restrictions
Species	Text	Donations to : Tigers, Rhinos, Orang-utangs, Turtles , Golden Eagles or No restrictions
DateLastDonated	Date/Time	Format DD/MM/YYYY
Amount	Currency	
SubscriberType	Text	Monthly, Quarterly, Annual or Occasional

Field Properties

General | Lookup

Field Size	2
Format	
Input Mask	
Caption	
Default Value	
Validation Rule	"UK" Or "AF" Or "AS" Or "SA" Or "XX"
Validation Text	Must be UK, AF, AS, SA or XX
Required	No
Allow Zero Length	Yes
Indexed	No
Unicode Compression	Yes
IME Mode	No Control
IME Sentence Mode	None
Smart Tags	

A field name can be up to 64 characters long, including spaces. Press F1 for help on field names.

Figure 10.7

 Enter an appropriate validation rule and validation text for the **Species** field. This field should only accept one of the values **TI**, **RH**, **OR**, **TU**, **GE** or **XX**.

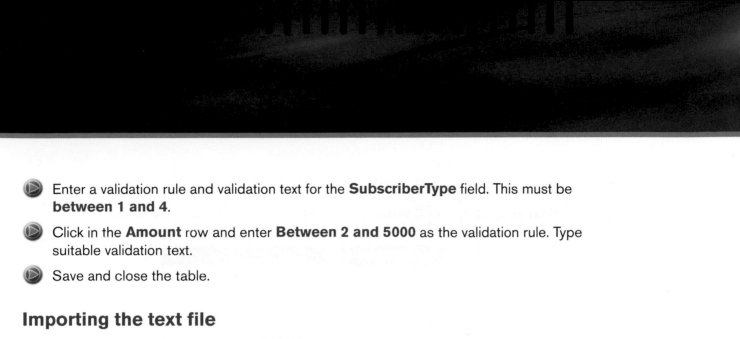

- Enter a validation rule and validation text for the **SubscriberType** field. This must be **between 1 and 4**.

- Click in the **Amount** row and enter **Between 2 and 5000** as the validation rule. Type suitable validation text.

- Save and close the table.

Importing the text file

Now you are ready to import the text file **GEADonors.csv** into your database.

- From the main menu select **File**, **Get External Data**, **Import**.

- Find the **GEADonors.csv** file that you have downloaded from the website.

 Tip:

You must specify **Text files (*.txt, *.csv, *.tab, *.asc)** in the **Files of type** box to see the file.

Figure 10.8

- Select the file and click **Import**.

- The **Import Text Wizard** appears.

Figure 10.9

Click **Next**.

 Click **Next** again to accept **Comma** as the character that separates the fields.

```
Import Text Wizard                                              [X]

What delimiter separates your fields? Select the appropriate delimiter and see how your text
is affected in the preview below.

┌ Choose the delimiter that separates your fields: ──────────────────────
│  ○ Iab      ○ Semicolon    ⊙ Comma      ○ Space      ○ Other: [    ]

☐ First Row Contains Field Names                  Text Qualifier:  {none} ▾

 1  Dr   K  Williamson   awilliamson9@aol.com       B16 ▲
 2  Ms   P  Boyles       brinboyles@tiscali.co.uk   OL1
 3  Mr   A  Henemulla    arizone@btinternet.com     NW1
 4  Mr   B  Robinson     chris@seaford.ac.uk        NG3
 5  Mrs  A  Rennie-Smith arenniesmith@lgfl.net      E14
 6  Ms   C  Walker       a.walker@yahoo.co.uk       ML5 ▼
◄                                                            ►

  [ Advanced... ]       [ Cancel ]  [ < Back ]  [ Next > ]  [ Finish ]
```

Figure 10.10

 Specify **tblDonor** as the table in which the data is to be stored.

 Click **Next**, and then click **Finish** in the next window.

 You should get a message telling you that the data has been imported; click **OK** to dismiss it. You can double-click **tblDonor** in the **Database** window to see the records.

You should have imported 200 records.

If you see an error message, check that you have defined all of the fields and specified the correct types for them; if, for example, you have specified that the **Species** field is numeric, none of the records will have been imported. Then check your validations; if you have specified **TG** instead of **TI** as the code for **Tiger** in the **Species** field then none of the tigers will have been imported, and you will have less than 200 records.

 Save and close the table and the database when you are satisfied all is correct.

Good marks... ✓

You will get good marks if you:

- download the data for the database and examine it carefully before you start designing the database structure;
- use meaningful field names, correct data types and suitable field lengths for the given data;
- include validations on fields where possible;
- import the given data and check that it has all been imported correctly.

Bad marks... ✗

You will lose marks if:

- you need help designing your database;
- you need help to import the data correctly;
- you have chosen wrong data types, unsuitable field names or unsuitable field lengths;
- you have not included sensible validation rules and validation messages;
- your database design is identical to someone else's.

Datasheet view

There are two ways to enter data in Access: one is to enter data into a table in **Datasheet** view, and the other way is to use a specially created form for data entry. We will start by looking at **Datasheet** view.

⊙ Open the **GEADonor** database and, in the **Database** window, double-click **tblDonor**.

At the bottom of the window you will see the **record selectors**, which can be used to go to a particular record or to go to a new record ready to enter more data.

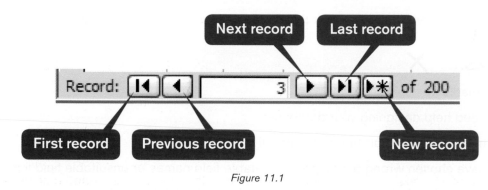

Figure 11.1

⊙ Click the **New record** button.

You will see the last few records in the table, and the cursor will be positioned ready for you to enter a new record.

DonorID	Title	Initial	Surname	Email	Postcode	Telephone	Daytime	Area	Species	DateLastDonated	Amount	SubscriberType
190	Ms	A	Chapman	chapmana@sion.org.uk	BN11 4BL	01903 267676	☐	UK	XX	30/09/2004	£25.00	1
191	Mr	C	Williams	c.williams@btinternet.com	EN1 1HQ	0208 360 3658	☐	AS	GE	19/08/2004	£10.00	4
192	Miss	P	O'Connor	p.oconnor@btconnect.com	NE63 0EF	01670 815690	☐	XX	XX	15/06/2004	£8.00	1
193	Mrs	D	Downey	d.downey@medway.co.uk	ME7 5TJ	01634 338500	☐	AS	TI	28/09/2004	£23.00	4
194	Mrs	C	chaudri	c_chaudri@hotmail.com	B33 9UF	0121 464 9765	☐	XX	TI	15/07/2004	£10.00	1
195	Mr	C	Shaw	chas.shaw@bournville.co.uk	B30 1QJ	0121 475 3381	☐	XX	XX	21/09/2004	£25.00	3
196	Mr	B	Richards	cmr@yab.richards@virgin.net	LL12 7AA	01978 315794	☐	AF	RH	15/02/2004	£25.00	3
197	Miss	A	Ingleby	ingleb@aol.com	PO5 3QW	02392 812118	☐	XX	XX	15/07/2004	£45.00	2
198	Mr	C	Lewis	clewis@hotmail.com	Cf47 9BY	01685 751726	☑	SA	XX	15/06/2004	£65.00	4
199	Mr	W	Byrne	w.byrne@tiscali.co.uk	CV32 6NB	01926 422416	☑	SA	OR	01/04/2004	£45.00	3
200	Mrs	A	Dinsmore	dddinsmore@hotmail.com	SE14 5SF	0207 6539500	☑	XX	TI	15/06/2004	£15.75	1
							☐				£0.00	0

Figure 11.2

⊙ Enter one or more new records. The first field is entered automatically for you, so just tab to the second field and type in some data.

Test out all your validations by attempting to type invalid data. For example, type **FR** in the **Area** field. When you tab out of the field, you should see your validation message appear:

Figure 11.3

Note that you can look at the structure of the table, and edit it if necessary, by pressing the **View** button on the toolbar.

Design View

Make any changes that are needed to the validation rules or their messages.

Save and close this table.

A more professional user interface can be created by designing a special form for data entry. The user can then use this form to enter records, though they can still enter and edit records in **Datasheet** view if they prefer.

Creating a data entry form

The easiest way to create a data entry form is to use a wizard.

In the **Database** window, click the **Forms** tab on the left-hand side of the window.

Select **Create form by using wizard**.

Figure 11.4: Preparing to create a form

Click the **New** button.

A window appears as shown in Figure 11.5.

 Select **Autoform: Columnar**.

 In the list box at the bottom of the screen select **tblDonor**.

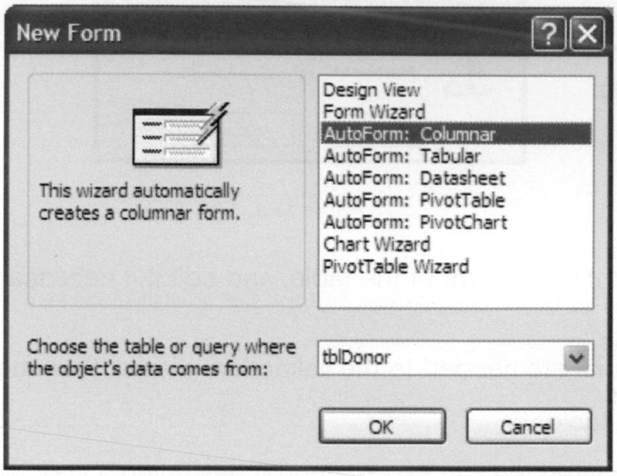

Figure 11.5: Creating a new form for tblDonor

 Click **OK**.

A new form is automatically created, and can be used for entering data.

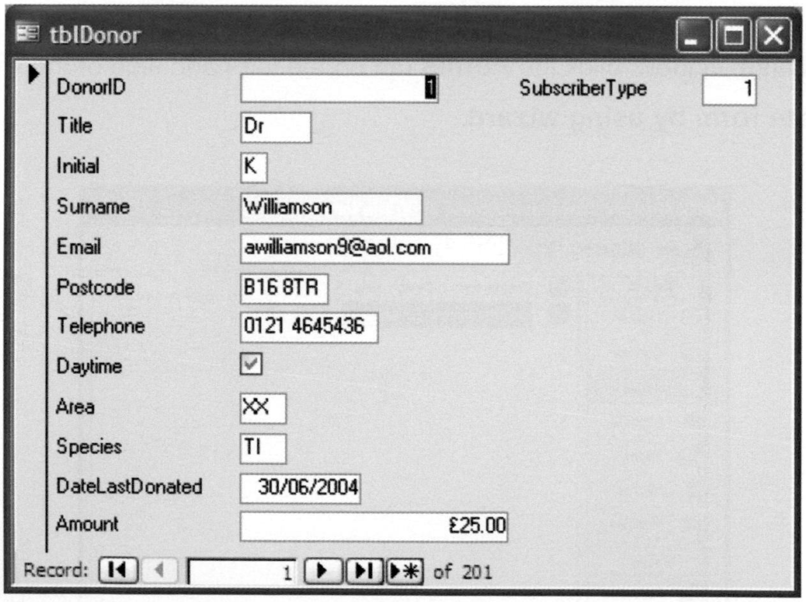

Figure 11.6: The data entry form created by the wizard

Customising the data entry form

All the items on the form, such as labels and text boxes where the user will enter data, are known as **controls**.

We could improve the form by:

- adding a heading;

- making the **DonorID** and **Amount** controls shorter;

- editing some of the field labels to make it clearer what the user is supposed to enter;

- adding a message to the **DateLastDonated** field to explain what format is expected;

- rearranging the position of the controls in a logical sequence;

- converting the **Title, Area** and **Species** fields to **Combo box** controls, from which the user can either select a value or type a new one;

- converting the **SubscriberType** field to an **Option Group** so that the user can select from the given options.

That's a lot of customising! There are other things you could do too, like changing the background or adding some graphics.

Enlarging the form

- Click the **View** button on the toolbar to switch to **Design** view.

- Enlarge the window so that you can see the edges of the form. Drag the right-hand side of the form to make it wider.

- Drag the top edge of the **Detail** section down to open a space for the **Form Header** section. We will put a heading in there.

Design View

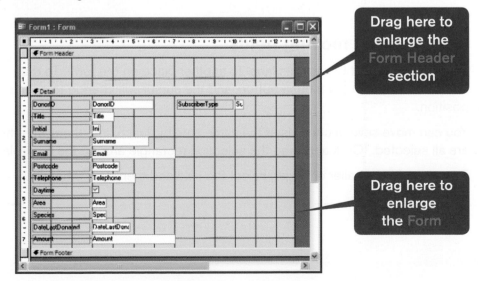

Figure 11.7: The form in Design view

Label

Inserting a label

▶ Click the **Label** tool and drag out a rectangle in the **Header** section. Type the text **Donors** in the box.

▶ Click the edge of the box to select it. Change the font to size **24**, **Arial**, **Bold**. Centre it and make it green or some other colour. You can make the **Fill** colour transparent or select a colour.

▶ Switch to **Form** view to see what it looks like, and adjust it if you are not happy.

⊞ tblDonor		_ □ ✕

Donors

▶	DonorID	[ ]1	SubscriberType	Q
	Title	Dr		
	Initial	K		
	Surname	Williamson		
	Email	awilliamson9@aol.com		
	Postcode	B16 8TR		
	Telephone	0121 4645436		
	Daytime	☐		
	Area	XX		
	Species	TI		
	DateLastDonated	30/06/2004		
	Amount	£25.00		

Record: |◀ ◀ 1 ▶ ▶| ▶* of 201

Figure 11.8: Form heading added

Resizing and moving fields

You can drag a text box and its label to another place on the form. To drag a field, click in the text box and hold down the mouse button, and the cursor will change to a hand. Drag it to the new position.

You can move several controls at the same time by 'lassooing' them with the cursor so that they are all selected. (Click and drag the selection rectangle around the controls you want to select.)

To make a field smaller or larger, select the field and then drag a handle.

Try moving and sizing the controls so that they are approximately as shown in Figure 11.9. We are going to be replacing some of the controls with combo boxes, list boxes and option groups.

Tip:

Use the bigger top-left handle to move the controls and their labels separately.

 Save the form, naming it **frmDonor**. The next time you save it, you could save it as **frmdonorV2**. Then you will be able to show your development work.

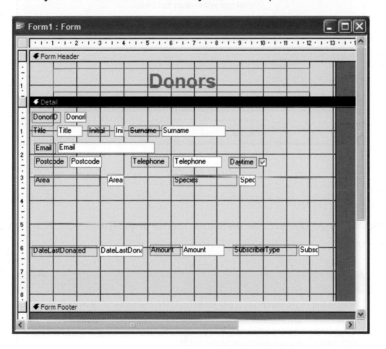

Figure 11.9: Moving fields around

Editing labels

You could add spaces to some of the labels like **DateLastDonated** and **SubscriberType**.

 Click the label and click again where you want to insert a space. Press the **Space bar**.

Inserting a combo box

We are going to replace the **Title** field with a **combo box**. (This is short for 'combination box' – you can either select from a list or type in a new value.)

 Click the **Title** field and press the **Delete** key to delete it.

 Click the **Control Wizards** tool on the **Toolbox**, if it is not already selected.

Control Wizards

In the **Toolbox**, click the **Combo box** tool. Click on the form where the **Title** textbox was. The **Combo Box Wizard** will appear.

 Click **I will type in the values that I want**.

Combo Box Wizard

This wizard creates a combo box, which displays a list of values you can choose from. How do you want your combo box to get its values?

○ I want the combo box to look up the values in a table or query.

⊙ I will type in the values that I want.

○ Find a record on my form based on the value I selected in my combo box.

| Cancel | < Back | Next > | Finish |

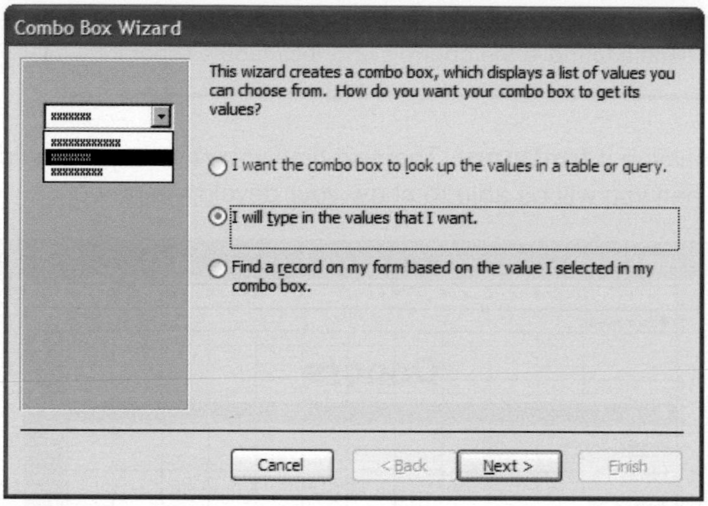

Figure 11.10

 Click **Next**.

 In the next window, type the values as shown, and any others you want to add. Also, make the column narrower.

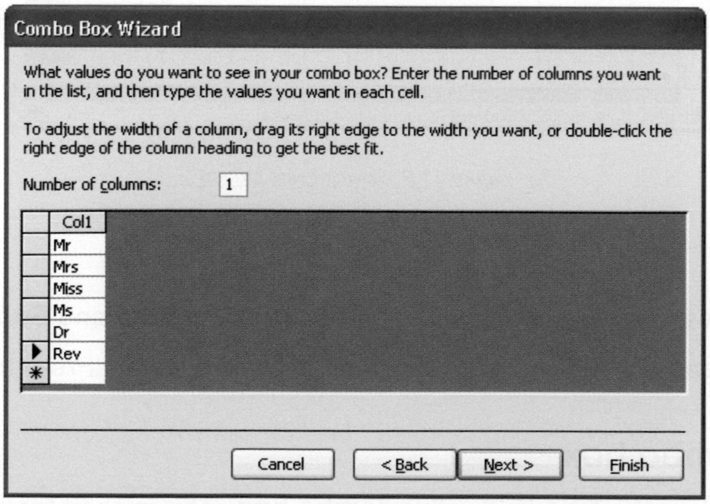

Combo Box Wizard

What values do you want to see in your combo box? Enter the number of columns you want in the list, and then type the values you want in each cell.

To adjust the width of a column, drag its right edge to the width you want, or double-click the right edge of the column heading to get the best fit.

Number of columns: 1

Col1
Mr
Mrs
Miss
Ms
Dr
▶ Rev
✱

| Cancel | < Back | Next > | Finish |

Figure 11.11

 Click **Next**.

 In the next window, specify that you want to store that value in the field **Title**.

Click **Next**. In the next window, specify **Title** as the label for the combo box. Click **Finish**.

Move the **Initial** and **Surname** fields if necessary to make room for the new combo box.

Go to **Form** view and use the **Record Selector** button to go to a new record. Click in the combo box to test it out.

New Record

Save your form.

Donors	

DonorID 1

Title Dr ⌄   Initial K   Surname Williamson

Email awilliamson9@aol.com

Postcode B16 8TR   Telephone 0121 4645436   Daytime ☑

Area XX   Species TI

Date Last Donated 30/06/2004   Amount £25.00   Subscriber Type 1

Record: |◄ ◄ 1 ► ►| ►✱ of 201

Figure 11.12

> **Tip:**
> You will probably notice that if you press **Tab** to leave the **AutoNumber** field, the **Title** field will be skipped over. We'll fix that later.

Inserting a list box

A list box differs from a combo box in that you can only select from the items listed – you cannot add a new value of your own. We will replace the **Area** control with a list box.

Delete the **Area** control.

In the **Toolbox**, click the **List Box** tool. Click on the form where the **Title** textbox was.

The **List Box Wizard** will appear.

List Box

Click **I will type in the values that I want**. Click **Next**.

Fill in the next box as shown in Figure 11.13.

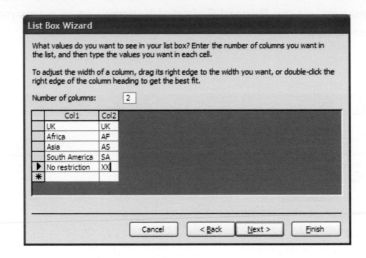

Figure 11.13

Click **Next**.

In the next window, specify that **Column 2** contains the value that you want to store in the database. Click **Next**.

In the next window, specify **Area** as the field to store the data in, and click **Next**.

In the next window, type the label **Area**. Click **Finish**.

Go to **Form** view and test out your new control by entering another record.

Now replace the **Species** control with a list box in the same way.

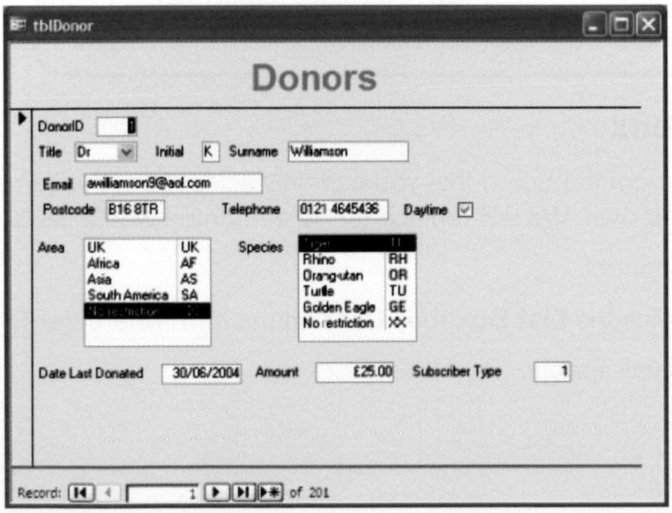

Figure 11.14

Inserting an option group

Next we will create an **Option Group** control for **Subscriber Type**. Note that you can only use an **Option Group** when the permissible values are numbered **1, 2, 3**, and so on. The user will be able to choose from options **Monthly, Quarterly, Annual** or **Occasional**. These values are coded **1, 2, 3, 4** in the data supplied.

Option Group

- Delete the label and text box for **Subscriber Type**.
- In the toolbox, click the **Option Group** tool.
- Click where you want to place the upper-left corner of the option group.
- Follow the directions in the wizard dialog boxes to add the four options.

Aligning fields

The form would look neater if the fields were lined up neatly.

- Hold down the left mouse button while you drag around the fields you want aligned. This is called "lassoing" them. You don't have to completely surround them to select them.
- From the **Format** menu select **Align**, and then select **Left**, **Right**, **Top** or **Bottom** depending on what you want to do.

Your form should look something like Figure 11.15 when you have finished.

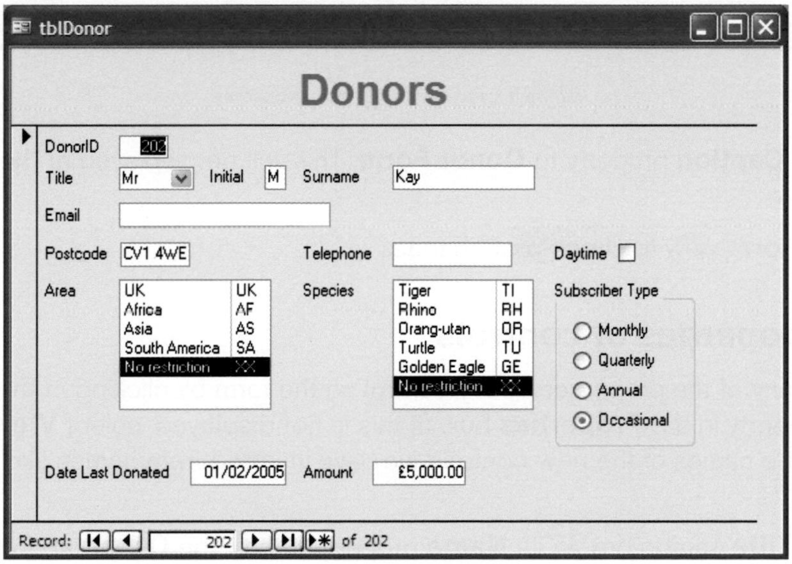

Figure 11.15

Changing form properties

Each control on the form, as well as the form itself, has numerous properties which you can change.

⊙ To display the form property box, double-click the small square at the intersection of the ruler lines.

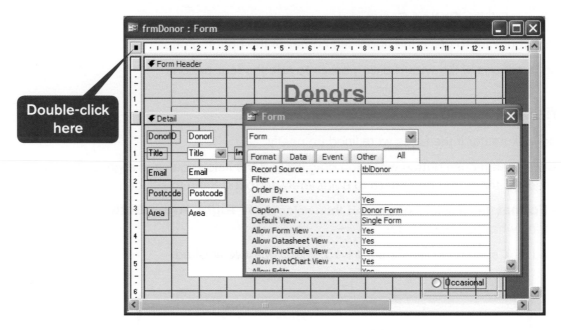

Figure 11.16: Displaying form properties

⊙ Change the **Caption** property to **Donor Form**. This will be displayed at the top of the form in **Form** view.

⊙ Change to **Form** view to check your change.

Changing properties of controls

You can change any of the properties of any control on the form by clicking in the control and changing the property in the **Properties** box. (If this is not displayed, select **View**, **Properties**.) We will change the names of the new controls we have inserted from names like **Combo27** to **Title**, and so on.

⊙ Click in the **Title** combo box. In its **Name** property (top of the **Other** tab in the **Properties** box), type **Title**.

⊙ Change the names of the other new fields.

You can change the **Status Bar Text** to give an explanation of the field. Look in the **Status Bar Text** property of the **Date** field – it tells you which format to use.

Changing the tab order

▶ Try tabbing through the fields in the form. The cursor skips all over the place, because we have deleted some controls and added new ones. We need to correct this.

▶ Make sure the form is in **Design** view.

▶ From the **View** menu select **Tab Order**. This brings up a window as shown in Figure 11.17.

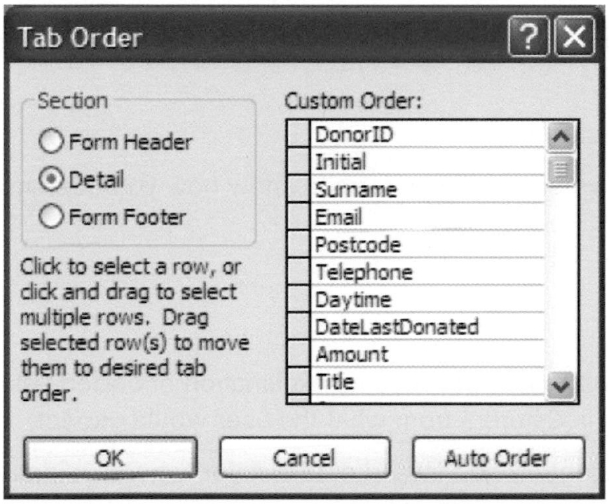

Figure 11.17: Changing the tab order

▶ Select the row containing **Title** by clicking in the grey selection box to the left of the name. Then click and drag to just under **DonorID**.

▶ Drag the other rows to rearrange them so that the user can tab sensibly from one field to the next without jumping about all over the place. Press **OK** when you have finished.

▶ Now test your form again.

▶ Save the form when you are satisfied.

You are now ready to test your form thoroughly!

Using the data entry form

▶ In **Form** view, enter some new records. Try entering some invalid data for the fields where you have set validations. You should see an error message displayed.

Tip:

You can always abandon a record by pressing **Esc**.

129

Good marks... ✓

You will get good marks if you:

- design a data entry form that is easy to use;

- include helpful features such as combo boxes, list boxes, option groups and Status bar messages;

- design a form that looks neat and attractive, with sensible headings and labels;

- test your form to make sure that a validation message is displayed whenever data is entered incorrectly;

- add new records correctly;

- keep at least two versions of your form to show how you customised it.

Bad marks... ✗

You will lose marks if:

- your form is difficult to use because no explanation of coded fields is included, or the tab order of the fields is different from what the user would expect;

- the user can accidentally add invalid data in fields where validations should be included;

- the form is difficult to read because the colours are not well chosen, the font is too small or fields are not visible because the form is too small;

- no customisation has been carried out.

What information do you think the charity would like to extract from the data they have collected? Here are some examples of the sort of information they might find useful.

1. **A list of the donors who can be telephoned during the daytime.** The report could include ID, title and surname, the date and amount of the last donation and whether they pay monthly, quarterly, annually or just occasionally. These people could then be telephoned to ask whether they would be prepared to subscribe on a regular basis or to increase their subscription.

2. **A list of people who contribute towards a particular species, such as tigers**, so that they can be sent a special newsletter about the work being done to save the tiger population from extinction. (The data in a real database would contain the full address of each donor so that they could be mailed.)

3. **A list of people who subscribe occasionally, but have not donated since 30/06/04.** This report could include their ID, title and surname, telephone number and whether they can be phoned in the daytime.

You can probably think of several other useful reports that could be produced from the data collected.

Creating a query

We will start by creating a query to find details of donors who can be telephoned during the daytime.

 Open the **GEADonor** database. In the **Database** window, make sure the **Queries** tab is selected.

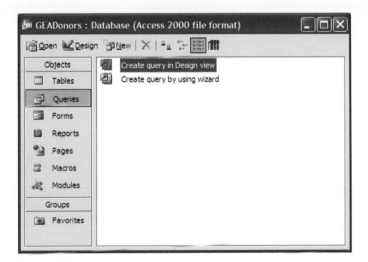

Figure 12.1

 Click **New**.

In the **New Query** window, click **Design View** and click **OK**.

 In the **Show Table** window, **tblDonor** will be selected. Click **Add**, then **Close**.

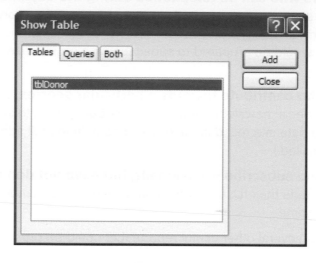

Figure 12.2

The **Query** window opens, showing the table in the top half of the window. You can enlarge the window and the **tblDonor** pane to show all the fields.

 Double-click each of the fields **DonorID**, **Title**, **Surname**, **Telephone**, **Daytime**, **DateLastDonated**, **Amount** and **SubscriberType** to put them into the query grid. Your query window should look like Figure 12.3.

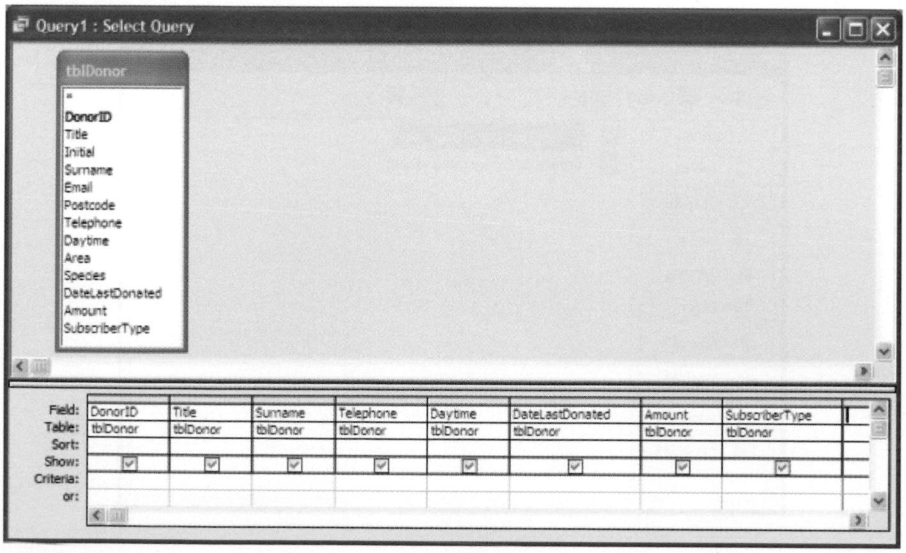

Figure 12.3

Tip:

You can adjust column widths by double-clicking between column headers.

In the **Criteria** row for **Daytime**, type **Yes**.

Save the query as **qryDaytime**.

Click the **Run Query** button. The query results will be displayed in a table.

Run Query

qryDaytime : Select Query

DonorID	Title	Surname	Telephone	Daytime	DateLastDonated	Amount	SubscriberType
1	Dr	Williamson	0121 4645436	☑	30/06/2004	£25.00	1
3	Mr	Henemulla	0208 8383426	☑	15/07/2004	£40.00	3
4	Mr	Robinson	01529 416195	☑	01/04/2004	£10.00	1
11	Mr	Manson	02881 676272	☑	15/06/2004	£25.00	3
12	Mrs	Grant	01540 662869	☑	30/06/2004	£20.00	1
13	Mrs	Johnson	020 8304 8627	☑	15/07/2004	£5.00	4
14	Mrs	Appleyard		☑	17/09/2004	£10.00	1
16	Mrs	Camfield	01757 701407	☑	15/06/2004	£15.75	1
17	Mr	Emenyeonu	0208 7673266	☑	01/04/2004	£10.00	1
20	Mr	Atkin	01249 717715	☑	05/10/2004	£45.00	3
21	Mrs	Chouder	0208 965 8481	☑	15/09/2004	£20.00	1

Record: ⏮ ◀ 1 ▶ ⏭ ▶* of 102

Figure 12.4

Sorting records

To sort the records, first return to **Design** view by clicking the **Design View** button.

In the **Sort** row click in the **Surname** column and select **Ascending**.

Design View

Field:	DonorID	Title	Surname	Telephone	Daytime	DateLastDonated	Amount	SubscriberType
Table:	tblDonor	tblDonor	tblDonor	tblDonor	tblDonor	tblDonor	tblDonor	tblDonor
Sort:			Ascending					
Show:	☑	☑	☑	☑	☑	☑	☑	☑
Criteria:					Yes			
or:								

Figure 12.5

Try running the query again. This time the records will be sorted alphabetically by surname.

133

	DonorID	Title	Surname	Telephone	Daytime	DateLastDonated	Amount	SubscriberType
▶	146	Mr	Alders	01952 598531	☑	15/02/2004	£50.00	3
	14	Mrs	Appleyard		☑	17/09/2004	£10.00	1
	152	Mr	Apthorpe	01246 432349	☑	25/09/2004	£35.00	4
	182	Mr	Astin	01756 791511	☑	29/09/2004	£45.00	4
	20	Mr	Atkin	01249 717715	☑	05/10/2004	£45.00	3
	158	Mr	Badger	01784 781994	☑	01/04/2004	£20.00	1
	66	Mr	Barker	01928 711353	☑	23/08/2004	£25.00	4
	53	Mr	Barzdo	0121 557 3837	☑	27/08/2004	£25.00	1
	67	Mr	Bedford	01928 721643	☑	13/09/2004	£60.00	4
	22	Mr	Bee	02920 250363	☑	15/02/2004	£20.00	4

Record: ◄◄ ◄ 1 ► ►► ►* of 102

Figure 12.6

 Save this query.

Saving a different query

We will make a second query, which will be similar to this one. Instead of starting from scratch, we'll save the first query under a different name and then edit it.

 From the main menu select **File**, **Save As**. Give the new query the name **qryDaytimeSortedbyType** and click **OK**.

Save As

Save Query 'qryDaytime' To:

qryDaytimeSortedbyType|

As

Query

OK

Cancel

Figure 12.7

Sorting on more than one field

Now suppose that we wanted to sort in descending order of **SubscriberType**, so that all the people who subscribe only occasionally appear first. Within each subscriber type, the records are to be sorted in ascending date order – in other words, the person who made a donation longest ago will appear at the top of the list.

 Back in **Design** view, change the **Sort** row in the **Surname** column to **(not sorted)**.

 Specify an **Ascending** sort in the **DateLastDonated** column, and a **Descending** sort in the **SubscriberType** column.

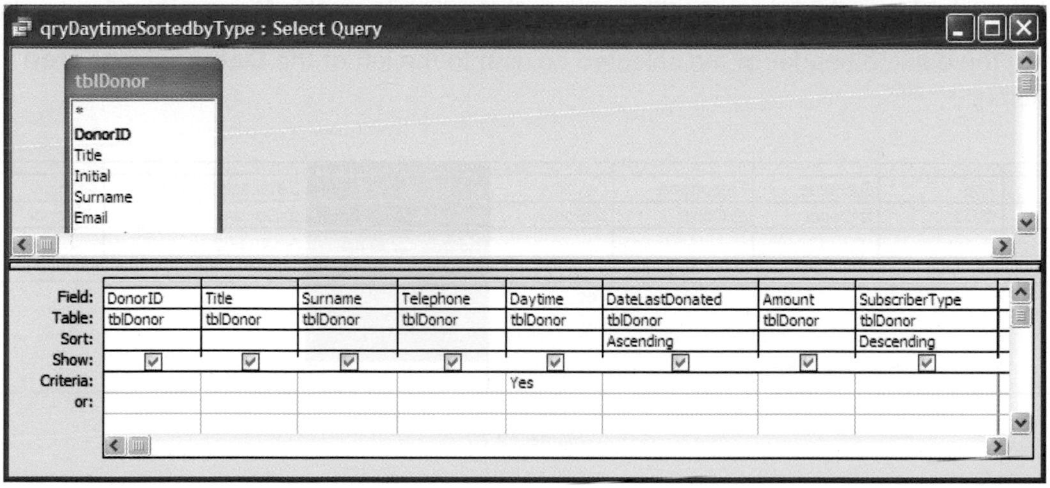

Figure 12.8

 Run the query.

The records have been sorted, but not quite in the order that we want. They are sorted in ascending order of **DateLastDonated**, and in descending order of **SubscriberType** within each date.

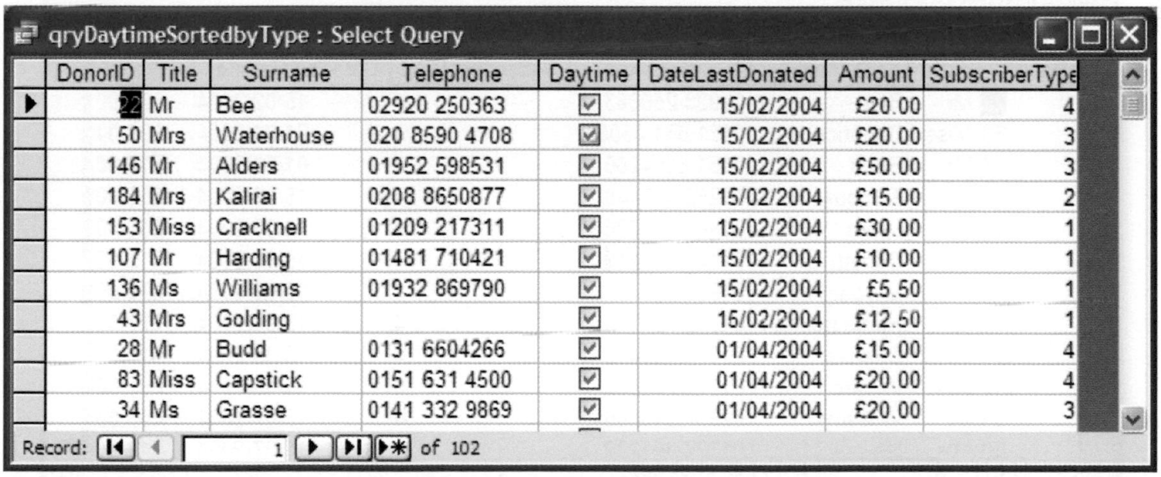

DonorID	Title	Surname	Telephone	Daytime	DateLastDonated	Amount	SubscriberType
22	Mr	Bee	02920 250363	☑	15/02/2004	£20.00	4
50	Mrs	Waterhouse	020 8590 4708	☑	15/02/2004	£20.00	3
146	Mr	Alders	01952 598531	☑	15/02/2004	£50.00	3
184	Mrs	Kalirai	0208 8650877	☑	15/02/2004	£15.00	2
153	Miss	Cracknell	01209 217311	☑	15/02/2004	£30.00	1
107	Mr	Harding	01481 710421	☑	15/02/2004	£10.00	1
136	Ms	Williams	01932 869790	☑	15/02/2004	£5.50	1
43	Mrs	Golding		☑	15/02/2004	£12.50	1
28	Mr	Budd	0131 6604266	☑	01/04/2004	£15.00	4
83	Miss	Capstick	0151 631 4500	☑	01/04/2004	£20.00	4
34	Ms	Grasse	0141 332 9869	☑	01/04/2004	£20.00	3

Record: 1 of 102

Figure 12.9

To fix this problem we need to change the order of columns in the query grid so that **SubscriberType** is to the left of the **DateLastDonated**.

Tip:

When more than one sort field is specified, records are sorted first on the leftmost field.

 Click the **Design View** button to return to **Design** view.

Click and release the mouse button in the column header of the **SubscriberType** column.

 Drag the column header of the selected column to the left of the **DateLastDonated** column.

DonorID	Title	Surname	Telephone	Daytime	SubscriberType	DateLastDonated	Amount	
tblDonor	tblDonor	tblDonor	tblDonor	tblDonor	tblDonor	tblDonor	tblDonor	
					Descending	Ascending		
☑	☑	☑	☑	☑	☑	☑	☑	
				Yes				

Figure 12.10

 Run the query again. This time the records should be sorted in the correct order.

Note that you can show or hide any field when you run a query. We don't really need to show the **Daytime** field, as we know they are all ticked.

 In **Design** view, click the **Show** row in the **Daytime** column to deselect it.

 Now run the query again. You should see the records as shown in Figure 12.11.

qryDaytimeSortedbyType : Select Query

DonorID	Title	Surname	Telephone	SubscriberType	DateLastDonated	Amount
22	Mr	Bee	02920 250363	4	15/02/2004	£20.00
83	Miss	Capstick	0151 631 4500	4	01/04/2004	£20.00
28	Mr	Budd	0131 6604266	4	01/04/2004	£15.00
180	Mr	Turnbull	01252 407448	4	15/06/2004	£10.00
198	Mr	Lewis	01685 751726	4	15/06/2004	£65.00
57	Mr	Canetti	0114 2723219	4	15/06/2004	£12.50
36	Mr	Morgan	01902 422 411	4	15/06/2004	£75.00
111	Mr	Harrington	01642 724413	4	15/06/2004	£23.55
181	Mr	Charles	01977 642442	4	15/06/2004	£10.00
145	Mrs	Wilson	01277 231588	4	15/06/2004	£55.00
33	Mr	Williams	020 75015160	4	15/07/2004	£55.00
60	Mrs	Newark	01327 301232	4	15/07/2004	£15.00

Record: ◄◄ ◄ 1 ► ►► ►* of 102

Figure 12.11

 Save and close the query.

Relational and logical operators

In the example above we asked Access to display only records which had '**Yes**' (equivalent to the checkbox being ticked) in the **Daytime** field. In other words, we set the criterion that **Daytime** had to be equal to **Yes**.

You can set more complicated criteria by using conditional and logical operators. Here is a list:

- Is equal to (=)
- Is less than (<)
- Is greater than (>)
- Is less than or equal to (<=)
- Is greater than or equal to (>=)
- Is not equal to (<>)
- AND
- OR
- NOT

The last three are called logical operators. For example you might want to find:

- all donors who subscribe monthly AND give an amount more than £5.00 each month;
- all donors who want their donations to go to rhinos OR turtles.

Multiple criteria

We will create a new query so that you can practise setting multiple criteria. We will start by finding all donors who subscribe monthly AND give an amount more than £5.00 each month.

- In the **Database** window, make sure the **Queries** tab is selected and click **New**.
- As before, use **Design View** and add **tblDonor** to the query window.
- Double-click each of the fields **DonorID**, **Title**, **Initial**, **Surname**, **Amount** and **SubscriberType** in turn to put them into the query grid.
- In the **Criteria** row's **SubscriberType** column, type **1**.
- On the same row, in the **Amount** column, type **>5**.

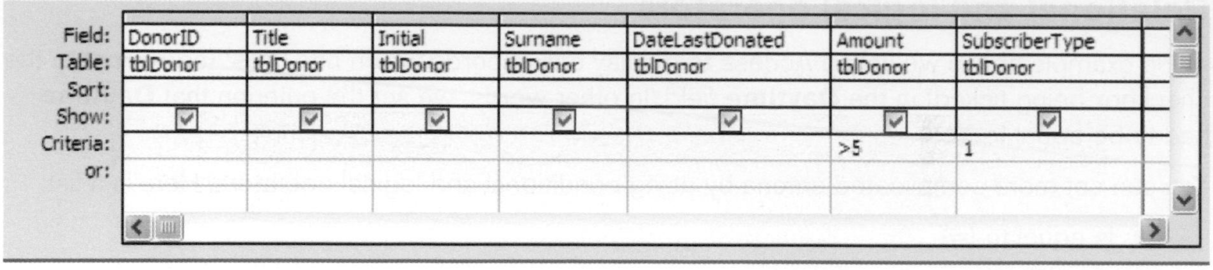

Field:	DonorID	Title	Initial	Surname	DateLastDonated	Amount	SubscriberType	
Table:	tblDonor	tblDonor	tblDonor	tblDonor	tblDonor	tblDonor	tblDonor	
Sort:								
Show:	☑	☑	☑	☑	☑	☑	☑	
Criteria:						>5	1	
or:								

Figure 12.12

 Run the query.

Your results should look like this:

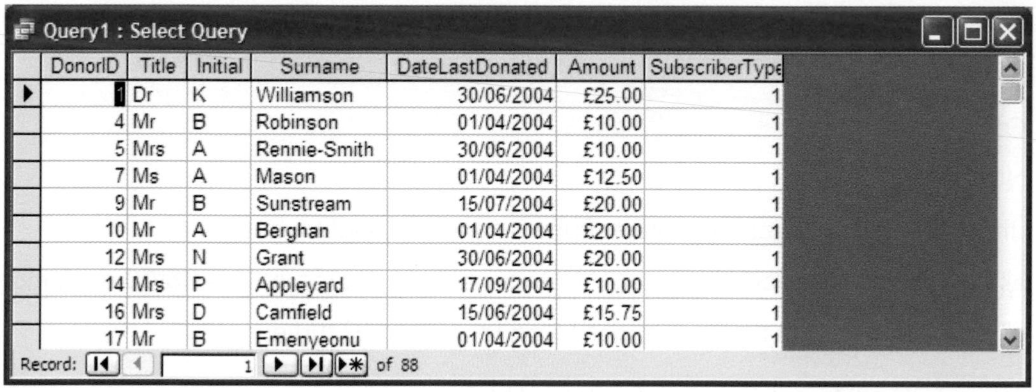

Figure 12.13

 Save this query as **qryMonthlyDonorsOver5**.

The OR operator

To find all donors who want their donations to go rhinos or turtles, you put the criteria on different lines.

 In **Design** view, add **Species** to the query grid.

 Change the criteria in the query you have just saved so that the query grid looks like this:

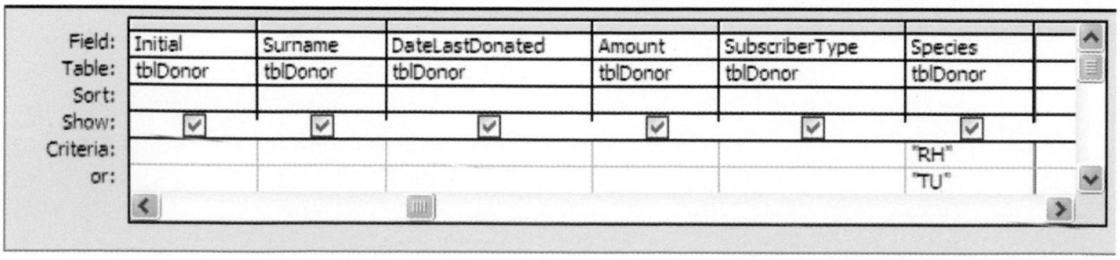

Field:	Initial	Surname	DateLastDonated	Amount	SubscriberType	Species	
Table:	tblDonor	tblDonor	tblDonor	tblDonor	tblDonor	tblDonor	
Sort:							
Show:	☑	☑	☑	☑	☑	☑	
Criteria:						"RH"	
or:						"TU"	

Figure 12.14

Run the query.

The result table should look like this:

DonorID	Title	Initial	Surname	DateLastDonated	Amount	SubscriberType	Species
8	Mrs	A	Rennie-Smith	30/06/2004	£10.00	1	RH
9	Mr	B	Sunstream	15/07/2004	£20.00	1	TU
10	Mr	A	Berghan	01/04/2004	£20.00	1	TU
11	Mr	C	Manson	15/06/2004	£25.00	3	TU
12	Mrs	N	Grant	30/06/2004	£20.00	1	TU
13	Mrs	C	Johnson	15/07/2004	£5.00	4	TU
22	Mr	T	Bee	15/02/2004	£20.00	4	RH
27	Mr	D	Fry	15/07/2004	£15.00	1	TU

qryMonthlyDonorsOver5 : Select Query

Record: 1 of 35

Figure 12.15

Select **File**, **Save As** to save the query, giving it the new name **qryRhinoAndTurtle**.

Close the query.

Good marks... ✓

You will get good marks if you:

- create queries that provide useful information;
- create queries that contain all the information you need to produce useful reports;
- use your plan.

Bad marks... ✗

You will lose marks if:

- your queries use the wrong criteria;
- you do not explain what the queries are for.

Information that is extracted from a database by using a query can be viewed on-screen, as in Figure 12.15 (page 139). However, it is often required in the form of a printed report, with a suitable title, column headings and so on.

Reports can be created either from the data in a table, or from data in a query results table. We will produce a report from **qryDaytimeSortedbyType**.

 In the **Database** window select the **Reports** tab and click **New**.

 Select **AutoReport: Columnar**, and **qryDaytimeSortedbyType** in the box below, as shown in Figure 13.1.

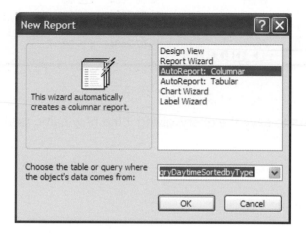

Figure 13.1

 Press **OK**. The report will be automatically created for you.

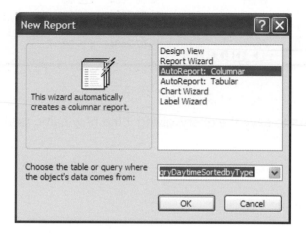

Figure 13.2

Tip:

Your report may look different from this. If so, select **Format**, **AutoFormat** from the main menu in **Design** view, and choose the **Corporate** style. Access will remember this choice as the default for future reports.

This is not a very convenient format, as it takes up so many pages. We will try an alternative method of generating the same report.

- Close this report without saving.
- In the **Database** window, click **New**.
- Select **Report Wizard**, and **qryDaytimeSortedbyType** in the box below. Click **OK**.
- Click the double-arrow between the two list boxes to select all the fields for the report.

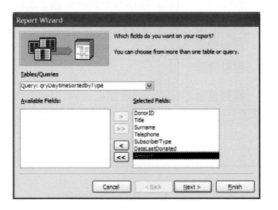

Figure 13.3

- Click **Next**.

In the next window, you can choose to have the report grouped under a particular field or fields. We will group the report by subscriber type.

- Select **SubscriberType** and click the arrow to specify a grouping level.

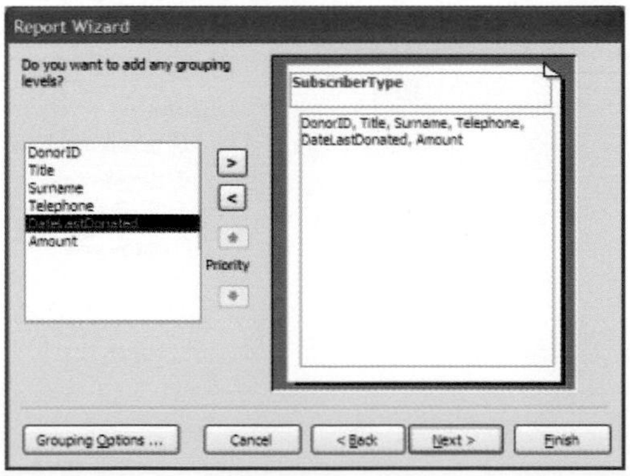

Figure 13.4

Click **Next**.

In the next window you can specify what order the records are to be sorted in. They will automatically be sorted in sequence by **SubscriberType**, because you have specified that field as a grouping level. Within each subscriber type, we can sort, for example, in descending order of amount. If two subscribers give the same amount, they will be sorted in alphabetical order of surname.

 Select **Amount** as the first sort field, and click the **Ascending** button next to it so that it changes to **Descending**. Select **Surname** as the second sort field.

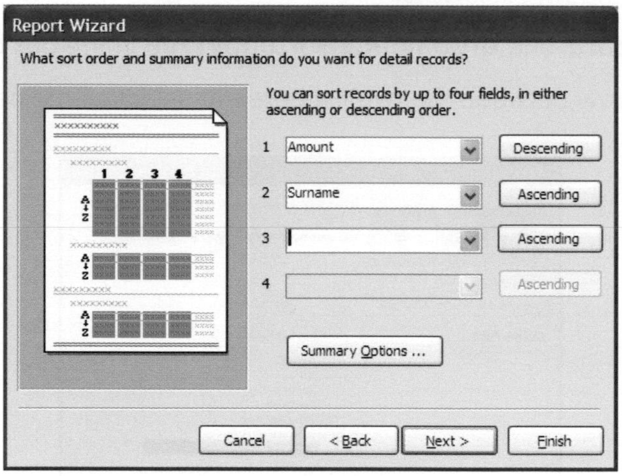

Figure 13.5

 Click the **Summary Options** button.

There is only one numerical field in this data, so Access gives you the option of calculating the sum, average, minimum and maximum of the **Amount** field.

 Click the **Sum** option and leave **Detail and Summary** selected.

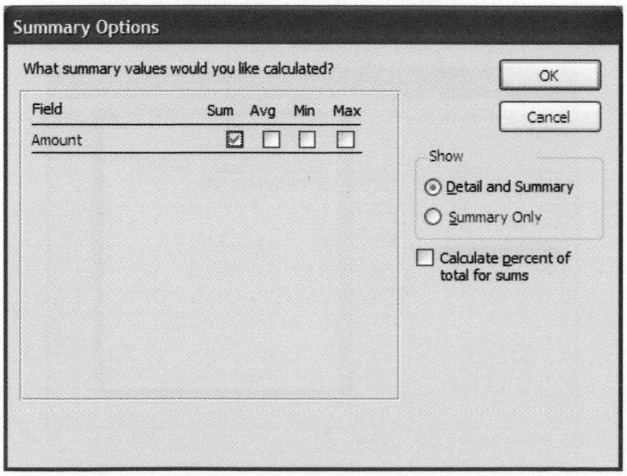

Figure 13.6

Click **OK** to close the **Summary Options** window. Click **Next** three times to select the **Stepped** layout and **Corporate** style.

In the final screen, give the report the name **rptDonorbySubType**. Click **Finish**.

The report will appear, looking something like this:

SubscriberType	Amount	Surname	DonorID	Title	Telephon	:LastDonated
1						
	£30.00	Cracknell	153	Miss	01209 21731	15/02/2004
	£25.00	Barzdo	53	Mr	0121 557 38	27/08/2004
	£25.00	Cheese	73	Mr	01424 21554	29/09/2004
	£25.00	Cooper	166	Mr	01487 99677	15/06/2004
	£25.00	Houghton	48	Mr	01578 75264	25/09/2004
	£25.00	Norris	78	Mr	07709 37581	29/09/2004
	£25.00	O'Leary	49	Mrs	01793 52739	20/09/2004
	£25.00	Seeley	186	Mr	02890 23641	15/07/2004
	£25.00	Williamson	1	Dr	0121 464543	30/06/2004
	£20.00	Badger	158	Mr	01784 78199	01/04/2004
	£20.00	Chouder	21	Mrs	0208 965 84	15/09/2004
	£20.00	Gould	85	Mrs	01795 58168	15/07/2004

Figure 13.7

There is a lot we can do to improve the appearance of this report and make it easier to interpret. For example:

- The report could be given a more explanatory heading.
- The columns could be re-ordered so that they appear in the sequence **DonorID**, **Surname**, **Title**, **Amount**, **Telephone**, **DateLastDonated**.
- The columns could be moved so that the headings are not truncated.
- The data could be lined up under the headings.

All of this can be done in **Design** view.

Modifying the report

Click the **Design View** button.

Click in the heading box and replace the text with a new heading, **Donors (Daytime telephone calls accepted)**.

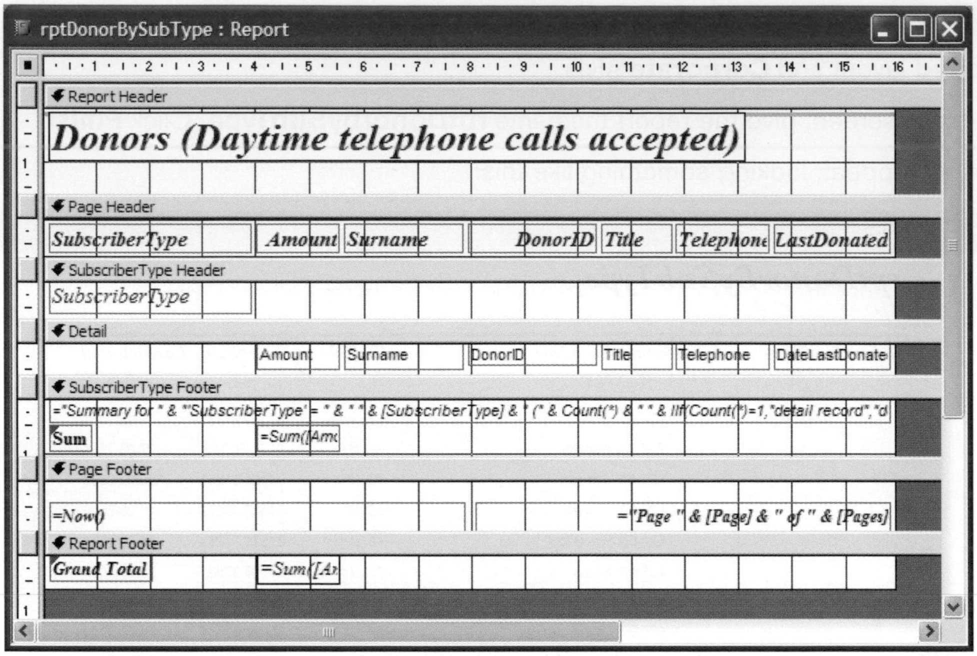

Figure 13.8

You can move the fields around on the report exactly as you can on a form. Remember that you can select and move more than one field at once by holding down the **Shift** key while you select multiple fields.

Try to get the report format to look something like Figure 13.9.

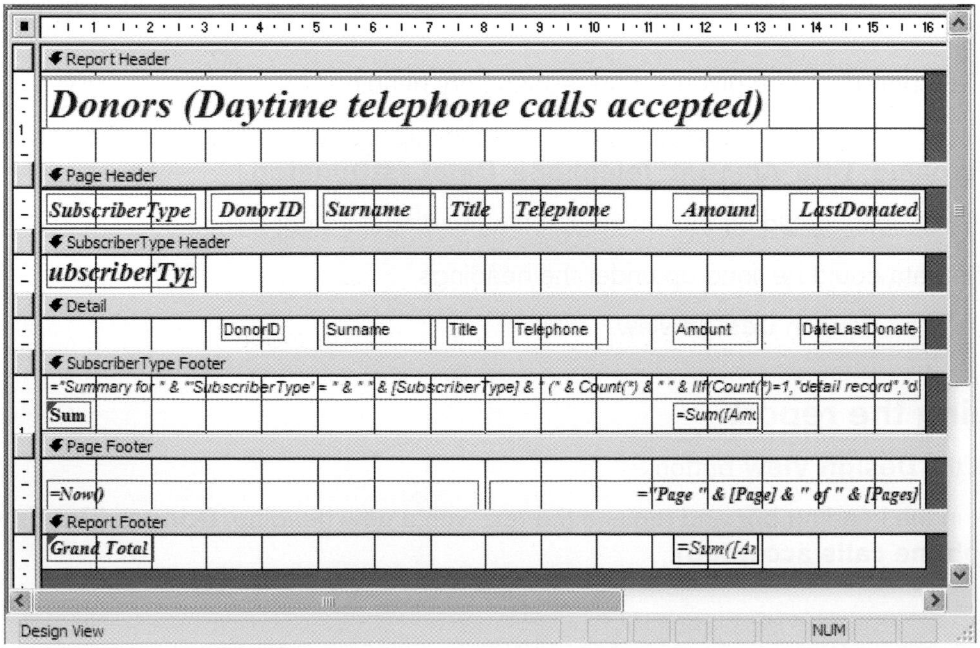

Figure 13.9

The report in **Print Preview** mode will then appear as shown in Figure 13.10.

Donors (Daytime telephone calls accepted)

SubscriberType	DonorID	Surname	Title	Telephone	Amount	LastDonated
1						
	153	Cracknell	Miss	01209 21731	£30.00	15/02/2004
	53	Barzdo	Mr	0121 557 38	£25.00	27/08/2004
	73	Cheese	Mr	01424 21554	£25.00	29/09/2004
	166	Cooper	Mr	01487 99677	£25.00	15/06/2004
	48	Houghton	Mr	01578 75264	£25.00	25/09/2004
	78	Norris	Mr	07789 37581	£25.00	29/09/2004
	49	O'Leary	Mrs	01793 52739	£25.00	20/09/2004
	186	Seeley	Mr	02890 23641	£25.00	15/07/2004
	1	Williamson	Dr	0121 464543	£25.00	30/06/2004
	158	Badger	Mr	01784 78199	£20.00	01/04/2004

Figure 13.10

Notice that totals are shown for each subscriber type, and a grand total is shown at the end of the report. You could remove the grand total, as it is not a very meaningful figure. It is a mixture of monthly, quarterly and annual subscriptions, and occasional donations.

 Return to **Design** view. Select the **Grand Total** label, and hold down the **Shift** key while you select the field on its right.

 Press the **Delete** key.

The **LastDonated** date might require some explanation too: you would need to know if it was the date that money was last received from a monthly subscriber, for example, or whether it was the date they pledged a monthly subscription, or last increased it.

You could add a text field at the bottom of the report to explain this.

Drag the bottom of the report down to make extra space.

Select the **Label** tool, and drag out a box at the bottom of the report.

Label

145

▶ Type text as shown in Figure 13.11.

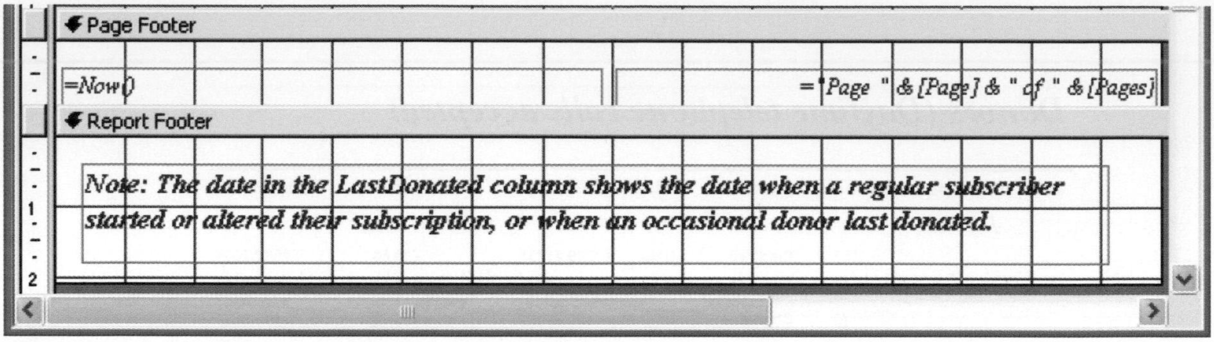

Figure 13.11

▶ Have a look at the report in **Print Preview**, and save and close it when you are satisfied.

▶ Try designing some useful reports of your own!

Good marks... ✓

You will get good marks if you:

- create reports that provide useful information;
- use sensible titles and column headings;
- sort and group the data into an appropriate and useful sequence;
- use subtotals and totals where appropriate;
- use your plan.

Bad marks... ✗

You will lose marks if:

- your reports do not make sense;
- the report title is meaningless, misspelt or absent;
- columns are badly positioned or do not fit across the page;
- the labels or data are truncated (cut off) because there is not enough room for them.

Chapter 14 – Concert Poster and Flyer

This chapter will take you through the processes involved in producing a poster and flyers designed to attract a crowd to the concert at the school.

You will take into account the following design considerations and techniques:

- using white space effectively;
- the different requirements for graphics in print and digital publishing;
- using a scanner and a digital camera to import images.

The software you will use to create the poster is Microsoft Publisher.

Before you start, look for sources of inspiration. The Internet is a good place. You could type **Rock Poster** into **Google Images** and see what ideas that gives you for layout and design.

Figure 14.1: Searching for ideas

Once you have an idea in your head, you should rough out a design on a piece of paper to give yourself something to work from.

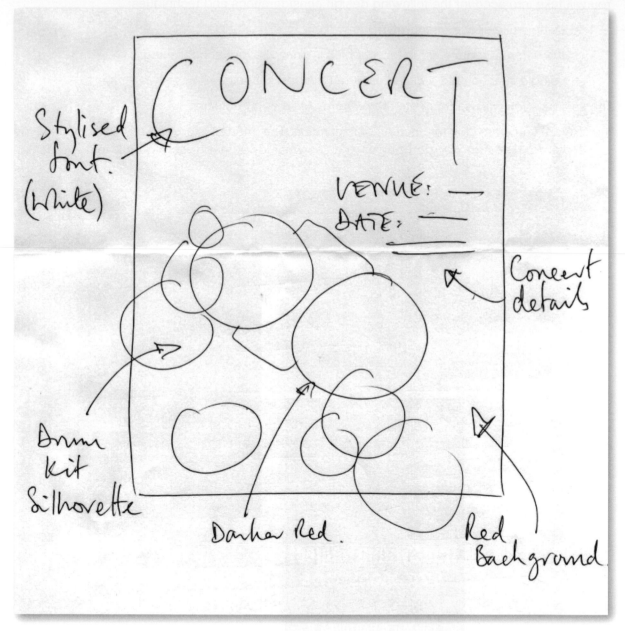

Figure 14.2: The hand-drawn design

▶ Load Publisher and select **Blank Print Publication** from the **New Publication** task pane.

▶ Close the task pane.

Checking the page setup

It is important just to check you have the right page setup before you start, otherwise you may finish the poster and find that it doesn't print as you expected it to.

 From the main menu, select **File**, **Page Setup**.

 On the **Printer and Paper** tab, check that the **Paper Size** is set to **A4** and that the **Orientation** is **Portrait**. Click **OK**.

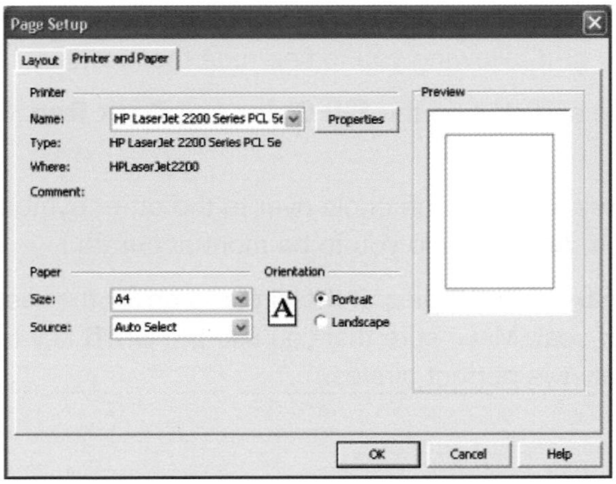

Figure 14.3: Checking the page setup

Creating a stylised image

You need to download two pictures from the website **www.payne-gallway.co.uk/didaD201** for this poster. The files that you need are **drumkitlayout.jpg** and **guitarist.bmp**. Save them in a suitable file.

 Select **Insert**, **Picture**, **From File** from the main menu, and insert the picture **drumkitlayout.jpg**. Resize it to fill the width of the page between the margins.

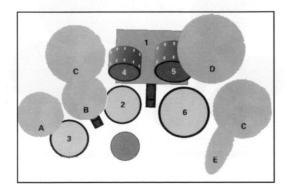

Figure 14.4

You could obtain images from a scanner, digital camera or the Internet. Make sure that if you use an image that isn't yours, you ask for permission to use it from the owner, and acknowledge them in your work.

You are only going to use this image as a template for creating a more stylised image of a drum kit. The actual image will not be included in the final poster.

Oval

▶ Using the **Oval** tool, draw a circle exactly over cymbal **C** in the left of the image. Hold down the **Shift** key while you drag out the shape to make it an exact circle.

▶ Keep adjusting it until it is right. Holding down the **Alt** key as well as **Shift** overrides PowerPoint's 'snap to grid', allowing you to fine-tune the size.

▶ Double-click the circle and change the **Fill Color** to a **Dark Red**. Set **Line Color** to **No Line** and click **OK**.

▶ Hold down the **Ctrl** key and drag the circle over to the other cymbal marked '**C**'. This should copy the circle. (Again, **Alt** may help you to be more accurate.)

▶ Use the **Ctrl** key to make more copies of the circle to cover the rest of the cymbals (except cymbal **E**), drums and seat. Make sure that you use the **Shift** key to resize them; this will ensure that they are always perfect circles.

> **! Tip:**
>
> You may find this easier if you change the **Zoom** to **Page Width** first.

Rotating objects

▶ For cymbal **E**, stretch the circle to a similar shape and size, then use the green **Rotate** handle to position the oval over the cymbal.

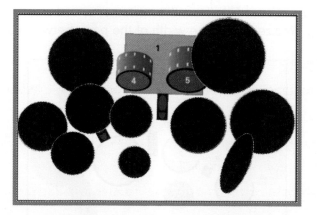

Figure 14.5: Using the Ctrl key to copy shapes

Can

▶ Now use the **Can** shape from the **AutoShapes, Basic** menu on the **Objects** toolbar to cover drums **4** and **5** in turn. Fill the Cans in the **Dark Red** too.

Tip:

By default, the can shapes will have ovals at the top (i.e. showing the top surface). To show the bottom surface instead, drag the bottom middle handle upwards until it is above the shape. You can also change the degree of 'tilt' using the yellow handle.

 Now use the **Rectangle** tool cover over drum **1** and the two foot pedals.

Rectangle

Managing the order of objects

You will notice that the large rectangle covers the drums.

 Right-click the large rectangle and select **Order**, **Send Backward**. Repeat this operation until it moves behind both the can shapes.

 Fill the seat in a slightly darker **Red**.

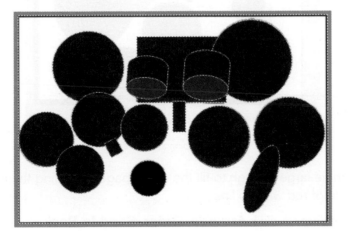

Figure 14.6

Grouping objects

All of these circles and rectangles can be grouped to form a single larger object.

 Click on the white area of the original image to select it.

 Press **Delete** on the keyboard. You should now be left with just the shapes you laid over it.

 With the mouse, drag a net around all of the objects.

 Click the **Group Objects** button that appears floating with the objects, or right-click the selection and choose **Group**.

 Now rotate the grouped object using the green **Rotate** handle, and position it as shown in Figure 14.7.

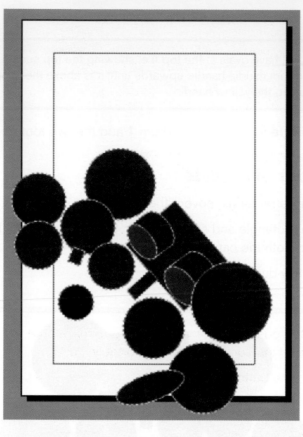

Figure 14.7: Grouping and rotating shapes

 Now add a rectangle large enough to fill the entire page, including the margins. Make this box a lighter shade of red with no line.

 With the box still selected, click **Arrange**, **Order**, **Send to Back**.

Adding the text

You should not add too much text to a poster. A poster is meant to grab your attention and give you all the information you need within a split second as you go past it. The text should be big, bold and easy to read from a distance, with the most important text being the biggest and most noticeable.

Text box

 Add a text box near to the top of the poster and type in **Painters**. This is the name of the band.

 Format the text as **Magneto** font, size **115** in **White**. If you do not have this font, select another appropriate font from your list.

 Use two more text boxes; put the word **The** in the first, and **Live** in the second.

 Format and position them as shown in Figure 14.8.

Figure 14.8: Adding striking text

 Group the three text boxes.

Now you need to check the positioning of your heading to make sure that it fits well on the page. You don't want it to hang off the edge or be uncomfortably close.

 Click the **Print Preview** button.

Print Preview

Figure 14.9: Using Print Preview

 Check that the band's name and the drum kit are sensibly positioned.

 Close the **Preview** window.

 If necessary, move the objects and check the preview again.

 Save the poster so far as **PaintersPoster.pub** under **Concert**, **Poster**.

 Add the rest of the text shown in Figure 14.10.

Using different fonts

The text box at the bottom of the poster uses the **Arial** font. This is so that the message here is differentiated from the rest of the information. It is an important message, but is not part of the information about the evening.

This is a good example of using different fonts. You should try to limit yourself to only two or three.

Figure 14.10

Using white space

White space is an area of the page with nothing on it (even if it is not white!). Having too many objects makes the page look cluttered and leaves no room for the objects on the page to 'breathe'. Often, white space is used to attract the eye in the first place. Having a large expanse of nothing makes people look closely to see what the poster is actually about.

Using white space gives a 'cleaner' final image – remember, 'less is more!'.

Creating an accompanying flyer

If you are putting up posters around the school to advertise a concert, you may feel that you need some flyers to support them.

The difference between a flyer and a poster is that a flyer is meant to be picked up and read at leisure. This means that you can add more informative text to it without worrying that it won't stand out enough.

This flyer will be to give to pupils at the school, who could use it, for example, to show their parents and ask for the price of a ticket.

Setting up the page

One advantage of flyers is that they are smaller than posters, so you can print several to a page.

- In Publisher, select **File**, **New** from the menu.

- Click on **Blank Publications**, then choose the **Postcard** style from the main window. Close the task pane.

- Now click on **File**, **Page Setup**. Click the **Printer and Paper** tab and set the **Orientation** to **Portrait**. Make sure that the **Paper Size** is set to **A4**, then click **OK**.

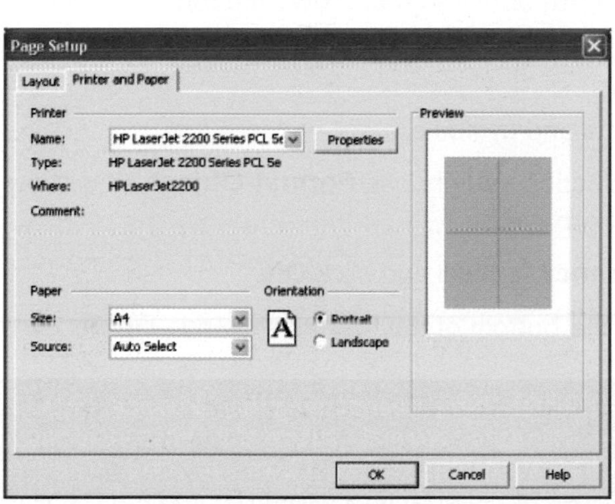

Figure 14.12

- Set out the flyer as shown in Figure 14.13. Copy and paste the text and drum kit design from the poster.

It is a good idea to make the flyer look very similar to the poster so that every time people see either a poster or flyer they will instantly associate it with the concert.

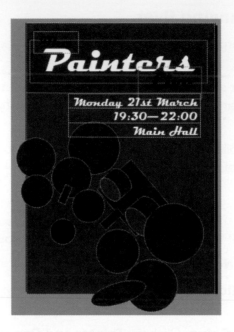

Figure 14.13

You are going to put some text about the band over the top of the drum design. With the current design it would be a little difficult to read, so the drum colours need to be softened or 'knocked back'.

- Select all of the drums and cymbals.

- Right-click on the selection and choose **Format Object**. (It will say **Format AutoShape** if the objects are not grouped.)

- Adjust the **Transparency** to **50%** and click **OK**.

- Now add the text to the bottom of the flyer as shown in Figure 14.14.

> The Painters have been touring the UK since 1999. They have released several successful hits including the number 1 smash 'Rolling Down' in 2003. Their most recent UK album 'Recovered' reached number 3 in the UK album charts and includes several of their latest hit singles.
>
> The band have kindly agreed to give a charity concert in aid of the GEA. This is a great opportunity to hear one of the UK's top bands in action.
>
> **Remember to bring £4.50 with you to school to book your ticket at Reception.**
>
> All proceeds will go directly to the GEA.

Figure 14.14

- Click the **Print Preview** button to make sure that everything fits on each of the four pages correctly.

- Save your flyer as **PaintersFlyer.pub** under **Concert**, **Flyer**.

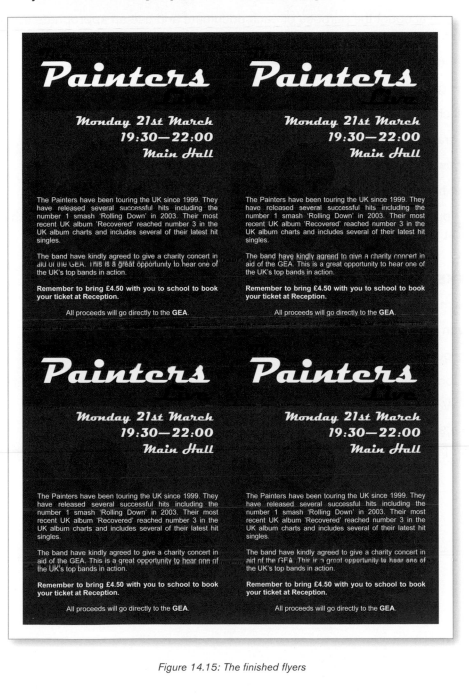

Figure 14.15: The finished flyers

Good marks... ✓

You will get good marks if you:

- plan your poster and flyer BEFORE you sit down at the computer;
- take into account the purpose of each document and use an appropriate size for each one;
- use fonts and font sizes consistently;
- make good use of white space;
- spell check and proofread your poster;
- use graphics at the right resolution;
- acknowledge copyright for images you have used;
- show how you responded to feedback from others and modified your work;
- use your plan. (You should tick off Tasks 14 and 15 and make notes about this task. Adjust your plan if necessary.)

Bad marks... ✗

You will lose marks if you:

- design a poster which is cluttered and has too much text;
- miss out important information on the poster or flyer;
- use too many fonts;
- use WordArt or clip art inappropriately;
- use irrelevant images;
- design a poster which looks the same as someone else's.

There are standard layouts for common paper-based documents used by individuals and organisations. You should know how to set out

- a letter;
- a report.

A business letter

Imagine that, as the person responsible for helping to organise the fund-raising concert at your school, you now have to write a letter to the band thanking them for giving their services, and telling them how much money was raised.

Purpose

Think first about the **purpose** of the document. What are you trying to achieve? The purpose could be, for example:

- to express your gratitude to the band for generously giving their time;
- to inform them how much money was made, and so make them feel that their efforts were worthwhile financially;
- to apologise for something that went wrong – the poor car-parking arrangements, lack of refreshments after rehearsal, power cut in the middle of the performance or some other setback.

However the concert went, if the audience enjoyed themselves then you probably want to make the band feel good about it so that you could invite them to play again!

Writing style

Next, think about the **writing style**. Is this to be a formal or an informal letter? Is the tone of the letter going to be matey, respectful, admiring, complaining? What is the age group and literacy level of the recipient? Is the recipient a child or an adult? A person of fame and status that you know only by reputation or someone you have known since you were best friends in Mrs Scott's reception class? The language that you use should be appropriate to the situation.

Layout

Standard documents have standard layouts. Business letters are often written on pre-printed stationery which has the name, address and telephone number at the top.

Using a template

Microsoft Word has templates for many different kinds of document, including letters, reports and newsletters. We will look at the letter template.

 From the **File** menu select **New**. The **New Document** task pane opens.

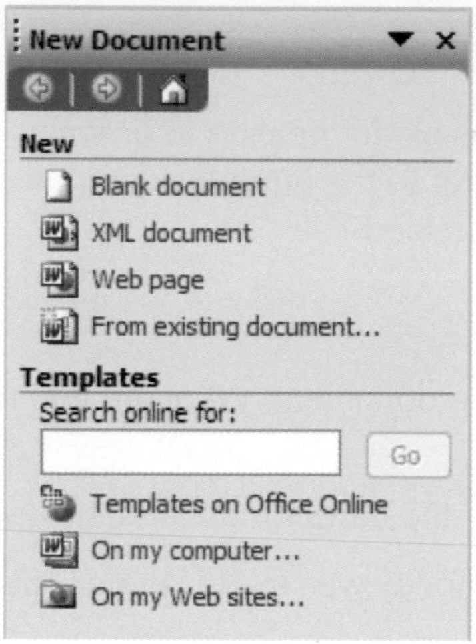

Figure 15.1

 Under **Templates**, click **On my computer...**

 You will see a dialogue box showing different templates. Click the **Letters & Faxes** tab.

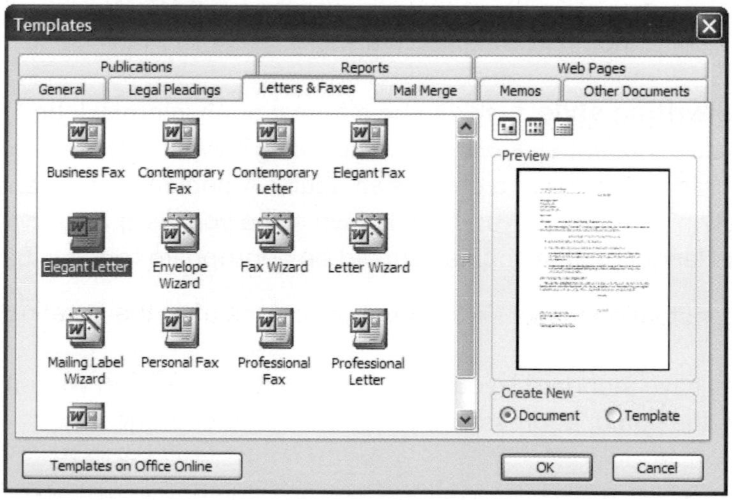

Figure 15.2

 Select **Elegant Letter** and click **OK**.

You will see the letter template on the screen.

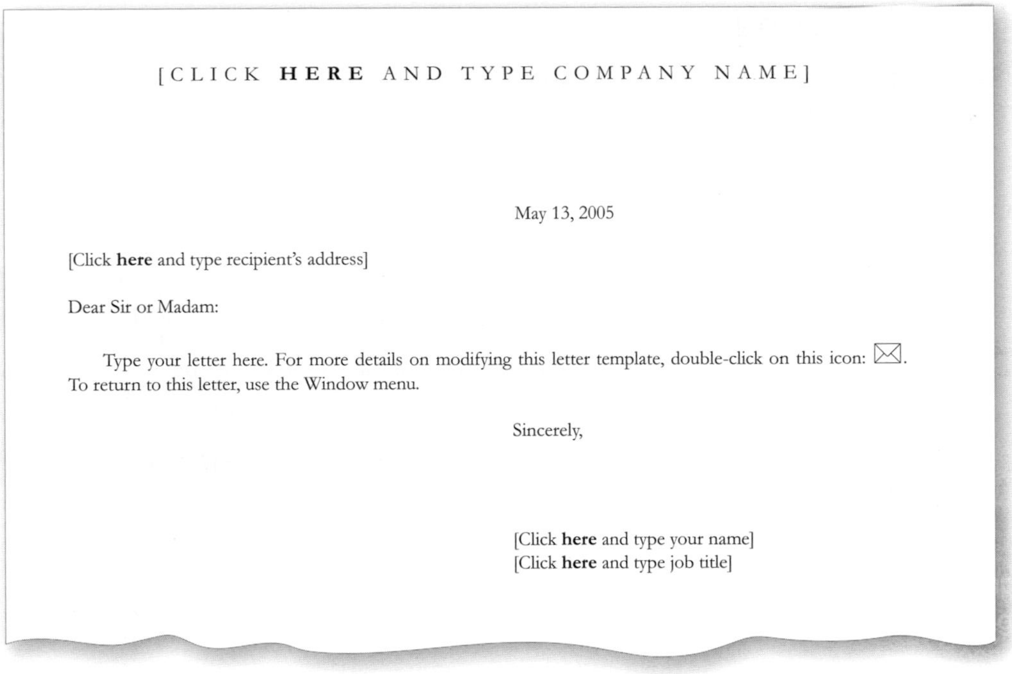

[CLICK **HERE** AND TYPE COMPANY NAME]

May 13, 2005

[Click **here** and type recipient's address]

Dear Sir or Madam:

Type your letter here. For more details on modifying this letter template, double-click on this icon: .
To return to this letter, use the Window menu.

Sincerely,

[Click **here** and type your name]
[Click **here** and type job title]

Figure 15.3

The address of the company appears at the bottom of the page, not shown in the screenshot.

Unfortunately, there is a lot about this template that does not conform to normal good practice in the UK. Some good rules to follow when writing a business letter are:

- Keep everything left justified.
- If the greeting starts **Dear Sir** then the closure should say **Yours faithfully**.
- If the greeting starts **Dear John** or **Dear Mr Cooper** then the closure should say **Yours sincerely**.
- Don't use punctuation marks like commas or colons after the greeting or the closure.
- Put a subject heading in bold under the greeting so that the recipient knows immediately what the letter is about.
- If you are replying to a letter which has a reference at the top, you should repeat the reference at the top of your letter, e.g. **Your ref: FC/jb**.
- If you are enclosing anything with the letter, put the abbreviation **Enc** under the name at the bottom of the letter.

You may be better off starting your letter from scratch, but we will amend this template and save a letter. If you want to modify the actual template, follow the instructions given when you double-click the envelope icon (shown in Figure 15.3).

Writing the letter

▶ Click at the top of the letter and enter the name of your school or college. Enter the address at the bottom of the page.

▶ Click where indicated and type the recipient's name and address (not just the address). You can make up a name and address or use the one in Figure 15.6.

▶ Replace **Sir or Madam** with the recipient's name.

▶ Select the date, and in the ruler line drag the indent symbol to line up with the rest of the letter against the left margin.

Figure 15.4

▶ Similarly, select the indented lines at the end of the letter and drag the indent symbol to the left margin.

▶ Select the first line of the body of the letter and drag the first line indent symbol in the ruler to the left margin so that the text is not indented.

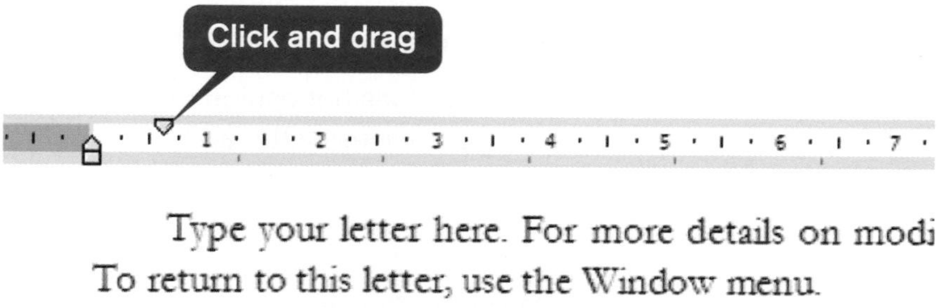

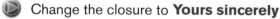

Type your letter here. For more details on modi
To return to this letter, use the Window menu.

Figure 15.5

▶ Type a subject heading and make it bold.

▶ Write the letter.

▶ Change the closure to **Yours sincerely**

▶ Type your name and job title where indicated.

Proofreading your letter

Before you print out your letter, you should look at it on the screen in **Print Preview** mode and check it thoroughly. Word will underline spelling mistakes in red, but it will not necessarily find all misspelt or wrong words so you need to read it through very carefully.

Check for grammatical, punctuation and formatting errors as well as factual errors.

Refer to Chapter 23 for more advice on proofreading.

Your letter should look something like this:

THE HIGHLANDS SCHOOL

25 March 2005

Mr James Halley
29 Penhayes Road
Exeter
Devon
EX12 4VG

Dear Mr Halley

Charity Concert 21st March

I am writing to thank you and all the Painters very much for so generously giving your time to raise money for the GEA. I am sure you could tell from the audience's reaction how much everyone enjoyed the evening.

You will be pleased to hear that the concert raised a total of £3,365, which is a record amount for a single fund-raising event at this school. We are all very encouraged by this and hope to put on more similar events in the future.

I am enclosing a write-up from the local newspaper, the Evening Star. I thought you might be interested to see it and their reporter is obviously a big fan.

Yours sincerely,

Belinda Harris
Chairman, School Fund-raising committee

Enc

Figure 15.6

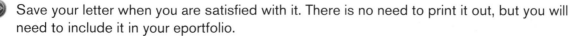

Save your letter when you are satisfied with it. There is no need to print it out, but you will need to include it in your eportfolio.

Refer to your plan, and tick off Task 16. Write any relevant notes about this task and check that you are still on schedule.

Writing a formal report

Writing a formal report is a challenging task. As with any other piece of writing, you should plan carefully, thinking about

- content and structure;
- components to be included, such as text, charts, diagrams, photographs;
- the proportion of text to visual information.

You also need to consider features such as

- headings and sub-headings;
- font type and size;
- line spacing.

Have a look at some formal reports on the Internet. For example, you could look at the Living Planet Report produced by the WWF.

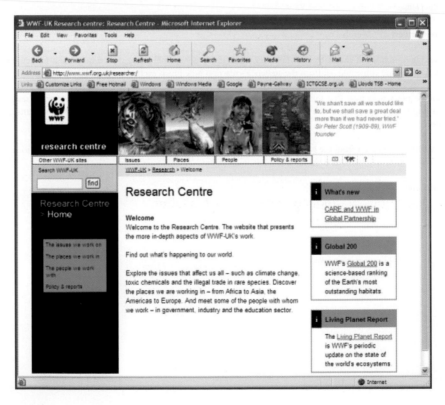

Figure 15.7: WWF website

Here are some tips for writing a formal report:

- Give the report a title.
- Start with an introduction which summarises what the report is about.
- Each separate topic in a formal report should have its own heading. Within a topic, you may have paragraphs with their own sub-headings.
- End with a summary, recapping the main points of the report.
- At the end, put a bibliography if you have used material from other people's work, from websites, books or magazines.

Good marks... ✓

You will get good marks if you:

- include all the standard components for each document;
- use a suitable style and content for your target audience;
- spell check and proofread your document.

Bad marks... ✗

You will lose marks if you:

- make mistakes of spelling or grammar;
- do not include standard components such as name, address and subject;
- do not use a correct greeting and closure in a letter.

Before you start building your eportfolio, you will need to make sure that

- you've planned the structure;
- you have everything you need to go in it;
- all of the files are in formats that can be viewed in a web browser (such as Internet Explorer).

What is an eportfolio?

An eportfolio is like a website which you will build to display all of your work. Each page will have a different piece of your work on it and may have links to other files, for example preparatory work, references or acknowledgments. Each page should also contain a link to the Home page, like a real website.

All the files which make up your eportfolio will be saved in the folder called **eportfolio** which you set up in Chapter 2.

What is the purpose of an eportfolio?

The purpose of an eportfolio is to showcase your work for the project. You need to make it as easy as possible for someone to view all the work you have done. It will function in the same way as a website.

It is a good idea to look on the Internet at other eportfolios that have already been created.

Try going to **www.google.com** and searching for **eportfolio**.

Have a look at some of the links for examples of what others around the world have created. You may find quite a few from America.

You could also look at the finished version of the one you will build in the next chapter: **www.payne-gallway.co.uk/didaD201/eportfolio**.

Who is going to see your eportfolio?

Your eportfolio will be seen by the assessor, who will probably be your teacher, and possibly by the moderator, who is appointed by the Exam Board. Your family or your class should also look at it to give you feedback so that you can improve it, but the finished product should be aimed solely at those who will be assessing your work. With this in mind, you need to make it very easy to find all the different components that you have created for the project. If the assessor can't find a piece of work immediately, he or she may move on without crediting you for it.

Remember:

You will be marked on every piece of work shown, and on the eportfolio itself.

Planning the eportfolio and creating a site map

Before you start designing anything on the computer, you need to have a clear plan in your head of how it will all come together. You need to plan the structure of the actual eportfolio. To start with, you will need a **Home** page (which must be saved as **index.html**) and a separate **Contents** page.

▶ Start by listing all the final components of the project that you need to include in the portfolio. This will give you the headings for your contents page.

1. Plan

2. File structure

3. Marketing leaflet for the GEA

4. Questionnaire for the survey

5. Analysis of the survey results

6. Presentation of the survey results

7. Interactive presentation for the GEA

8. Database of all the donors

9. Poster and flyer for the band and concert

10. Letter of thanks to the band

11. Evaluation of the project

> **Tip:**
>
> When you create your eportfolio for the Edexcel SPB, check the Edexcel website for a list of everything that you must include.

You will also need to add several pages to show the stages you took in implementing the various components, any references or acknowledgements you need to make and details of any feedback you received and improvements you made.

You already have a folder called **cportfolio** oot up to hold tho cito. We will now add subfolders to this folder to hold the various elements that you will select and prepare to go in the eportfolio. For example a subfolder called **PosterandFlyer** could contain the final pdf versions of the poster and flyer, and some early versions (converted to pdf files) to include in your evidence.

▶ Create the following subfolders within your **Eportfolio** folder: **MarketingLeaflet**, **Analysis**, **ResultsPresentation**, **InteractivePresentation**, **PosterandFlyer** and **BandLetter**.

Now that you have made a list of contents, you can sketch out the structure of the eportfolio. It might look something like this:

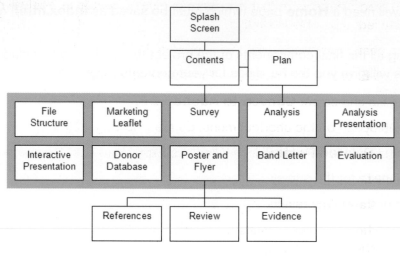

Figure 16.1

You may change these plans as you begin to build the actual portfolio, but you do need to have something in mind that you can begin to work with.

Preparing your files

You will need to prepare some of your files so that they can be opened in a web browser, such as Internet Explorer, even if the viewer does not have the actual piece of software that you used to create the file. For example, you can save a PowerPoint show so that it can be viewed by people who do not have PowerPoint on their computers.

You will also need to make sure that each file you include in your eportfolio is saved as one of the types allowed by the Edexcel specification. These are:

.pdf	Adobe's Portable Document File
.html or .htm	Hypertext Markup Language web file
.swf	Macromedia Flash file
.ppt	PowerPoint file
.gif	Graphics Interchange Format (image file format)
.jpg	Joint Photographics Expert Group (image file format)
.png	Portable Network Graphics (image file format)
.wmv	Windows Media Video
.wav	Wave file (audio file format)

Figure 16

 Save in the **Eportfolio\ResultsP**

Your file will now have a different icon a PowerPoint.

 Repeat this operation for the **GEA**

 Remember to save two or three ea supporting evidence.

Saving an Excel spreadsheet as

Your survey results collected in Excel n you can save the spreadsheet as a wel the need for Excel to be loaded.

 Open the latest version of your an

 Select **File**, **Save as Web Page** option is selected.

Figure 16.5: Co

Creating an Adobe PDF file

Files created in Word or Publisher can easily be converted into pdf files. Pdf stands for Portable Document Format, which means that the converted files can be read by anyone, even people who don't have the piece of software that they were originally created in. You will need to have Adobe Acrobat installed to be able to do this.

We will convert the poster and the flyer into two separate PDF files.

 Open **Windows Explorer** and select the **PaintersPoster** file.

 Right-click the file and select **Convert to Adobe PDF**.

If you do not get this option on the shortcut menu, do the following instead:

 Double-click the **PaintersPoster** file in Windows Explorer to load the poster in **Publisher**.

 Select **File**, **Print**.

 Set the **Printer Name** to **Acrobat Distiller**.

 Click the **Properties** button and select the **Adobe PDF settings** tab. Select **eBook** in the **Conversion Settings** and click **OK** twice.

Figure 10.2. Creating a PDF file

 Save the file in the **Eportfolio\PosterandFlyer** folder.

The file will be converted and **Adobe Reader** should open to display your file.

● Convert one or two
  the **Supporting E**

● Repeat this operat

● Save pdf versions

● Save pdf versions

Creating a self-run

In order for the interacti
without PowerPoint you

● Load **PowerPoint**

● From the **File** men
  PowerPoint Sho

Evaluation

Plan	**The eportfolio**
File Structure	**This is an evaluation of the final version of my eportfolio.**
Marketing Leaflet	**Outcomes**
Survey Questionnaire	I created the eportfolio in Word and checked it thoroughly using the following criteria:
Analysis of Survey Results	
Presentation of Survey Results	
Interactive Information Point	
Database of Donors	
Concert Poster and Flyer	
Letter to the Band	

Outcomes
I created the eportfolio in Word and checked it thoroughly using the following criteria:
- The whole portfolio has a consistent appearance
- The navigation buttons are in the same place on each page
- The layout is logical and easy to follow
- All the links work correctly
- Every page loads up quickly
- Most pages are short enough not to require excessive scrolling
- Spelling and grammar is correct

I referred to my plan while building the portfolio to ensure that all components were included.

Suggestions for improvement
It might have been better to have a separate link in the navigation bar for Evidence of development. The Evidence page could be bookmarked for each item.
Each page could have a 'Back' button taking the user back to the page previously visited. However, the user could use the existing button on the Internet Explorer toolbar.

Process
I underestimated the time it would take to do the questionnaire, analysis and presentations and I had to adjust my schedule. I also forgot to write down where I downloaded some of the images from and it took a long time to find them again.

Figure 18.3: The top of the Evaluation page

Good marks... ✓

You will get good marks if you:

- keep referring back to your plan and objectives to see if you met them;

- describe who each component is for, and consider whether it does its job;

- ask others for feedback and consider carefully whether you agree with it, and, if so, respond to it;

- make suggestions for how you could improve your project.

Bad marks... ✗

You will lose marks if you:

- do not refer to your plan;

- do not get feedback from others;

- do not show how you acted on the feedback, if it was appropriate.

Section Two
RESEARCHING INFORMATION

This unit is concerned with using ICT to

- plan,
- research,
- analyse, and
- present information

through work on a major project set by Edexcel.

In the next few chapters we will look at the different ways which you can use to research the information you need for a particular project.

Information sources

There are many ways of finding out information. For example you might use:

- ICT-based sources, such as the Internet, an intranet, CD-ROM or teletext;
- a paper-based source, such as a newspaper, magazine, brochure, encyclopaedia, directory or manual;
- a questionnaire that you have devised and handed out to people.

Discussion:

Where would you look up information on each of the following? Give a different answer for each one.

1. **Train times to Edinburgh**

2. **Arsenal's position in the Football League tables**

3. **What's on at the local cinema**

4. **The number of mountain gorillas living in the wild**

5. **A good deal on a laptop computer**

6. **Information on meteorites for a science project**

7. **The correct spelling of the word 'practice' (or is it 'practise'?) in the sentence "He is going to *practi–e* his saxophone for an hour tonight."**

8. **Holiday offers in Majorca**

9. **Ways to save money on the cost of heating a home**

10. **Where to find a particular book in the library**

Of course, you can find out almost all of these on the Internet. What an amazing source of information it is! But equally amazing is the fact that a large section of the population has never used the Internet and yet they still manage to conduct their daily lives quite happily, and find out all sorts of useful information.

Primary and secondary sources

Any research project involves gathering information for particular purposes, such as:

* to increase knowledge;
* to help with decision-making;
* to make recommendations.

You can use a wide range of information sources, both **primary** and **secondary**.

When you use information that has been produced by someone else, you are using a secondary source. Secondary sources include:

* paper-based sources such as newspapers, directories, books, maps;
* ICT-based sources such as the Internet, CDs or DVDs, databases;
* TV and radio.

You will have to select the most appropriate secondary sources, by asking questions such as:

* Is it unbiased?
* Is the information reliable and up-to-date?
* Can it be trusted?

Bias

Information is said to be **biased** if it is one-sided or expresses an opinion that does not reflect the entire situation or event that took place. A biased account of an event is unbalanced and will often be written to reflect the author's opinion, missing any information that may conflict with what they want you to believe or the message they want to get across.

For example, consider a football game between Ipswich Town and Norwich City where the score was 2-1 to Ipswich. After the match, two post-match reports are posted, one on each of the official websites. It is likely that the Norwich report would be written by a team fan, who may claim that the match was very much theirs and it was just an unlucky result. The Ipswich fan, on the other hand, may write that it was an absolute trouncing and that Norwich were lucky to get even one goal!

It would be sensible then, if researching this game, to dismiss both reports as biased.

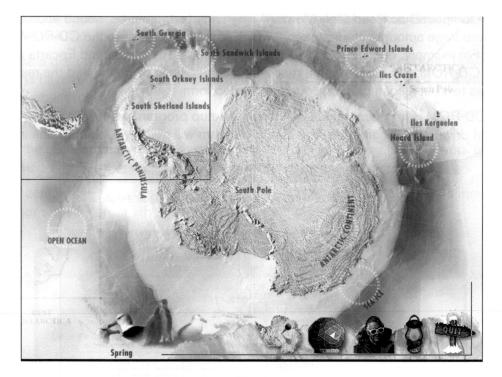

Fig 22.2: A CD-ROM about the Antarctic

Here, for each of the four seasons, you can view a panorama of a zone and click in circled zones to find out more about the wildlife there.

Figure 22.3: Life around the sea ice

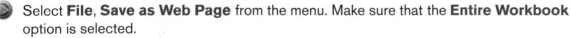

Figure 16.4: Creating a PowerPoint Show file

 Save in the **Eportfolio\ResultsPresentation** folder.

Your file will now have a different icon associated with it, and should open and run without PowerPoint.

 Repeat this operation for the **GEAInformationPoint** presentation.

 Remember to save two or three early versions as PowerPoint shows to include in your supporting evidence.

Saving an Excel spreadsheet as a web page

Your survey results collected in Excel need to be viewed by the assessors. To assist them in this, you can save the spreadsheet as a web page. This will allow them to open it in a browser without the need for Excel to be loaded.

 Open the latest version of your analysis spreadsheet in Excel.

 Select **File**, **Save as Web Page** from the menu. Make sure that the **Entire Workbook** option is selected.

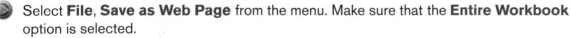

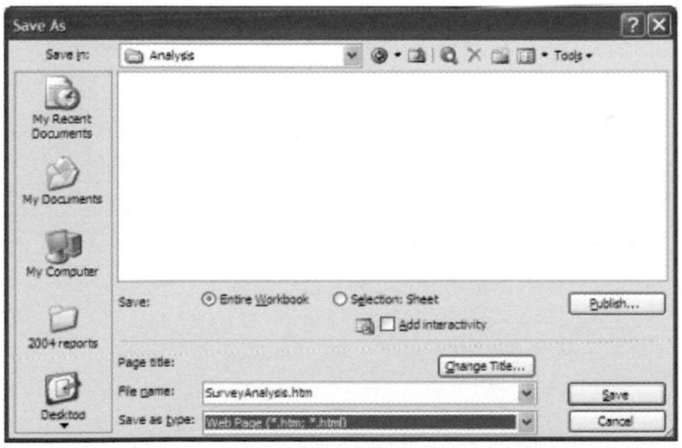

Figure 16.5: Converting a spreadsheet file into a web page

⊚ Save the file as **SurveyAnalysis** and put it in the **Eportfolio\Analysis** folder. This will automatically give you the new web-compatible spreadsheet file and another folder containing several more files that Excel has created.

Taking screenshots

A screenshot is an image of your screen. Throughout this book screenshots, such as the one shown in Figure 16.5, have been used to demonstrate what is happening.

The database cannot be converted into a suitable format for the assessor. Instead, you will need to capture images of the database screens to put directly into your eportfolio. You will also need to take screenshots of other things to include, such as your folder structure in Windows Explorer.

There are several ways you can include screenshots. Either you may have access to a special piece of software used specifically for grabbing images of the screen, or you could simply use the **Print Screen** (**Prt Scr**) button at the top right of your keyboard.

When you press this button, an image of the screen is stored in the **Clipboard**. You can then press **Ctrl+V** or **Edit**, **Paste** to insert the image into your document. Try this exercise to see how it works:

⊚ Open a new Word file.

⊚ Press **Print Screen** on the keyboard.

⊚ Now select **Edit**, **Paste** from the menu.

You should see the image of the whole screen pasted into your new document.

⊚ Now select **File**, **Open**. This should open a smaller window on the screen.

⊚ Now press **Alt+Print Screen**.

⊚ Click **Cancel** on the **Open** window.

⊚ **Paste** the screenshot into the document under the other one.

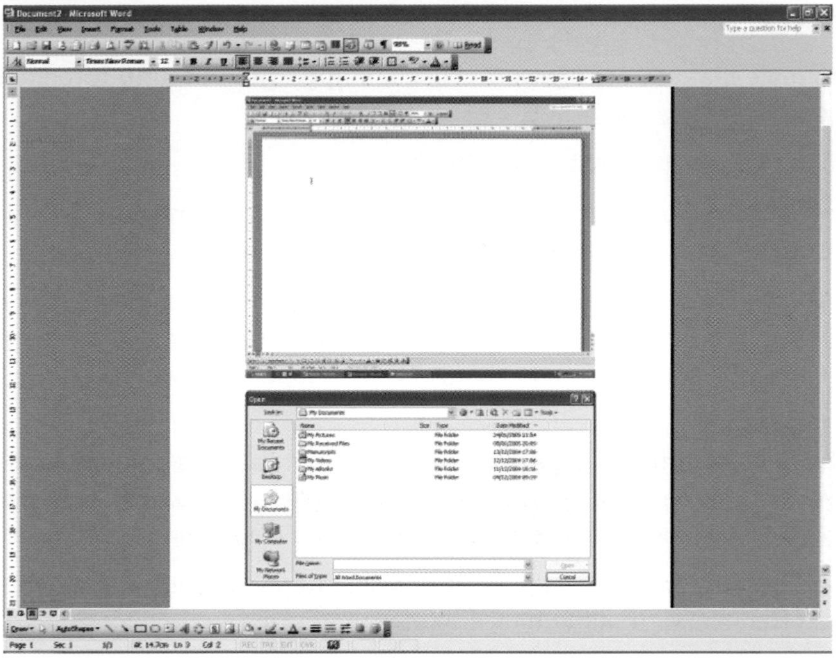

Figure 16.6: Taking screenshots

The important difference is that **Alt+Print Screen** will take a picture of just the active window. This makes the overall file size smaller and, in the case of an eportfolio, faster to download.

You can also use the **Crop** function on the **Picture** toolbar to shave off any unnecessary areas of the screen image, although this won't reduce the actual file size of the image.

▶ Close the file without saving.

Each page in your eportfolio will itself be a Word document, so you will be able to paste the screenshots you need straight into the appropriate page. (See Figures 17.16, 17.22, 17.23 in the next chapter.)

Using a screen capture utility

Screen capture software is readily available and comes as part of many graphics packages. You can also download free software from the Internet. The software will enable you to save your images as files and then if necessary, you can import them into a graphics package to crop them or convert them to an image format suitable for your eportfolio.

For printed work you need to take screenshots at a resolution of 300dpi, but this will result in large files. For your eportfolio a resolution of 72dpi is sufficient.

Image formats

The image file formats that you are allowed to use are **.jpg**, **.gif** and **.png** (pronounced '*jay-peg*', '*giff*' and '*ping*' respectively).

To decide when to use which format, follow this basic guide:

A **.jpg** file is most suitable for photographs, graphical artwork and images with a lot of colours. Jpeg files are compressed, making them relatively small.

.gif images are also compressed, but can only handle a small number of colours, so they are most suitable for non-photographic images such as logos or black and white images. gifs also have the ability to handle animations and images with transparent backgrounds, which jpegs cannot.

.png files are the newest format. They are similar to gifs but they are able to handle millions of colours. They were developed to help replace the gif format, and are now widely supported by the Web, though they will never completely take over since they cannot support animation.

Your images need to have the smallest file size possible while still retaining a good quality, so that they will load fast. Remember that the total size of your eportfolio must not exceed 15Mb.

Chapter 17 – The Eportfolio

The eportfolio will be created in Word. Each part of the portfolio will be saved as a web page; these will eventually all be linked together according to the plan in Chapter 16. To see a finished example of the eportfolio, visit the Payne-Gallway web site at **www.payne-gallway.co.uk/ didaD201/eportfolio**.

The first page that you will see in a website is the **home page**. For an eportfolio this is a title page which will have your name and candidate details on it.

▶ To begin making your first page, open a new document in **Word**.

Setting up the page

Before you start doing anything, you will need to change the view of the page in Word to show how it will look as a web page.

▶ Click **View**, **Web Layout** on the main menu.

Starting to develop a web page using tables

Tables are the best way to lay out a web page. They allow each element on the page to be positioned accurately.

▶ Using the menu options **Table**, **Insert**, **Table**, insert a table **2 Columns** by **4 Rows**.

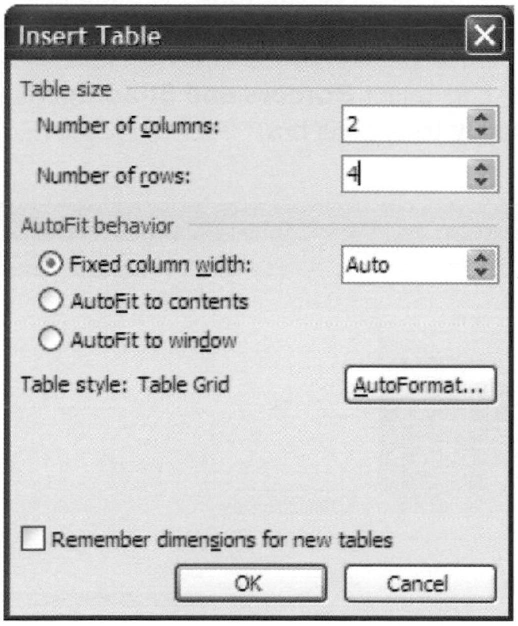

Figure 17.1: Inserting a table

⊙ A table will appear. Using the mouse, drag the borders of the cells to adjust the dimensions of the table as shown in Figure 17.2.

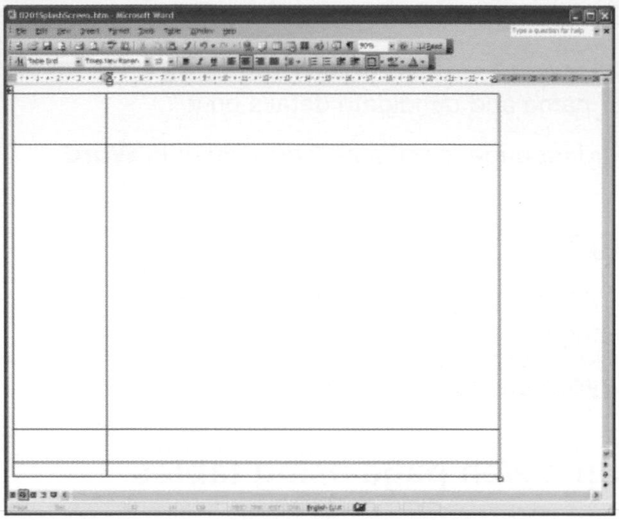

Figure 17.2: Adjusting cell borders

⊙ Highlight the cells on the top row and select **Table**, **Merge Cells**. This will create a banner across the top of the page in which you can write the page title.

⊙ Do the same with the third and fourth rows.

⊙ Right-click in the top cell and select **Borders and Shading**. Select a **Dark Blue** shade and select **Cell** in the **Apply to** options box.

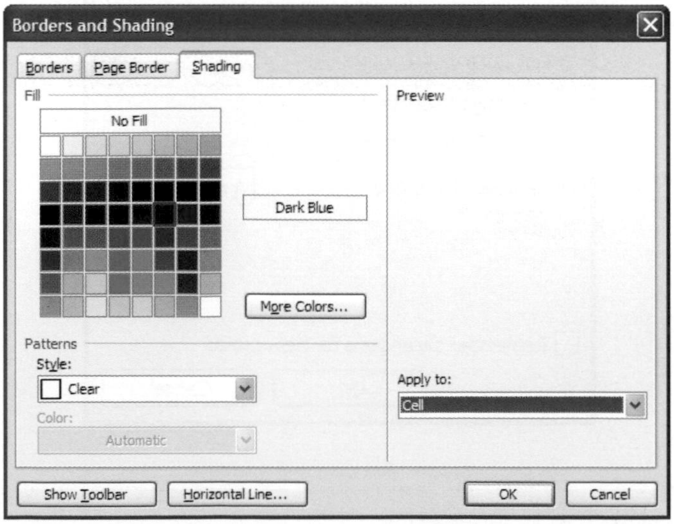

Figure 17.3: Adding shading to a cell

⊙ Click **OK** to apply the new colour to the cell.

Shade in the other cells as shown in Figure 17.4.

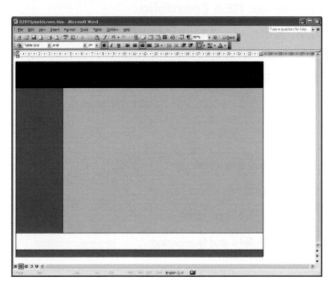

Figure 17.4

Saving a file as a web page

 Click **File**, **Save as Web Page** on the main menu. You will save all the pages that you create in the **Eportfolio** folder that you have already set up.

Tip:

The Home Page must be called **index.html** (all in lower case) and saved in your project folder, not the Eportfolio folder.

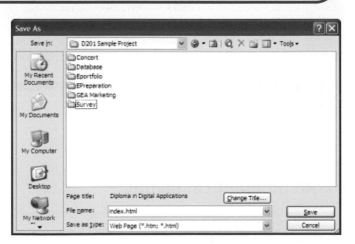

Figure 17.5: Saving a file as a web page

Name the file **index.html** and ensure that the **Save as type** option is set to **Web Page** **(*.htm;*.html)** and **not Single File Web Page (*.mht;*.mhtml)**.

Inserting text into a cell

 In the top banner enter the text **GEA Eportfolio**.

 Format the text as **Arial**, **Bold**, size **34**.

Aligning objects in a cell

 Right-click in the cell with the title and select **Cell Alignment**. Click the **Align Center Right** button.

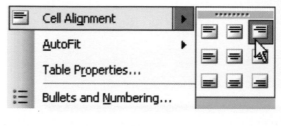

Figure 17.6: Aligning text

 Enter the rest of the details, as shown in Figure 17.7. You can replace them with yours if you wish!

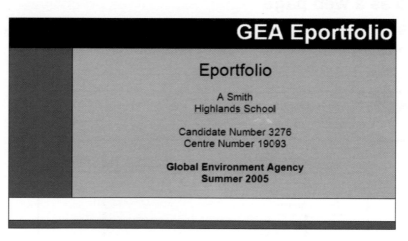

Figure 17.7

 Save the page.

Creating a page with an identical layout

Once you have saved the page you can then save it again under a different filename. This will keep the same look and dimensions, meaning that nothing will seem to jump around when you move from one page to the other.

This is important because you will be awarded higher marks if your pages look consistent.

▶ Select **File, Save As Web Page**. Name the file **D201Contents**, make sure the **Save as type** is set to **Web Page**, and click **Save**.

This will create an identical file with the new name. You now need to transform this page into the contents page.

▶ Make the following alterations to the text and colours and save the page again.

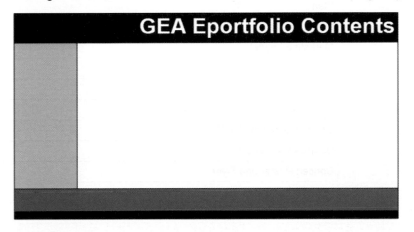

Figure 17.8

Splitting a cell into more rows and columns

The large main cell needs to be split into several more rows, one for each item in the eportfolio.

▶ Without selecting any text, right-click the large cell and select **Split Cells**.

Figure 17.9: Splitting cells

▶ Select **1 Column** by **11 Rows**, since there are 10 content pages shown in the site map in Figure 16.1, and we must also link to the plan. Click **OK**.

Enter the contents headings shown in Figure 17.10. Make them **Arial**, size **18**, **Blue** and align them **Center Left**.

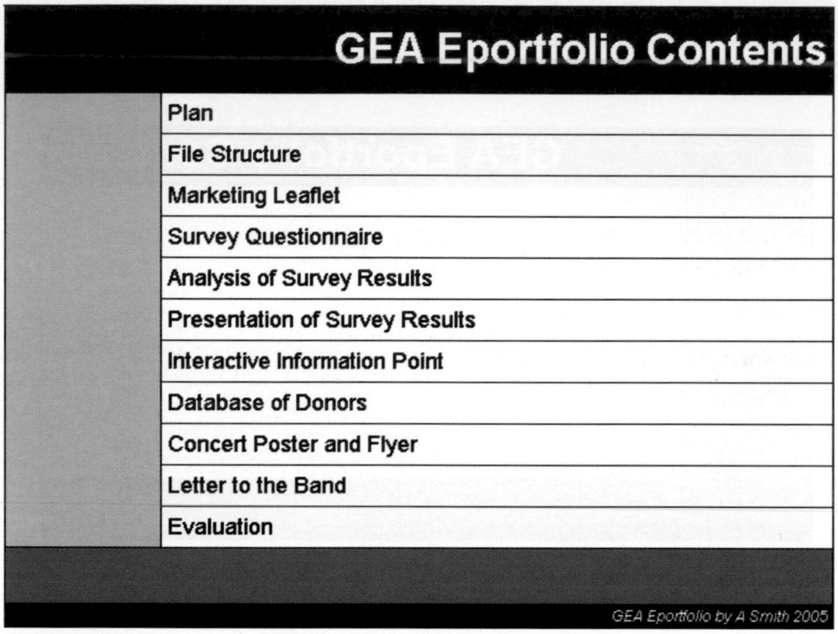

GEA Eportfolio Contents

Plan
File Structure
Marketing Leaflet
Survey Questionnaire
Analysis of Survey Results
Presentation of Survey Results
Interactive Information Point
Database of Donors
Concert Poster and Flyer
Letter to the Band
Evaluation

GEA Eportfolio by A Smith 2005

Figure 17.10

 Save the page again.

Creating buttons

To create a button you first draw a shape and then apply a hyperlink to it. Alternatively, you could find an image of a button on the Internet and add a hyperlink to that.

 From the main menu select **Tools**, **Options**. In the **General** tab, make sure that **Automatically create drawing canvas when inserting AutoShapes** is not ticked, then click **OK**.

Drawing

 Make sure that the **Drawing** toolbox is visible by clicking on the **Drawing** button in the **Standard** toolbar.

Rectangle

 Use the **Rectangle** tool to draw a box on the right of the medium blue banner at the bottom of the page.

 Format the shape **Dark Red** with **No Line**.

Shadow

 Use the **Shadow** tool to make a faint shadow under the button (**Shadow Style 17**).

● Right-click the rectangle and select **Add Text**. Type **Go Back to Student Details**. Format the text as **Arial**, **Bold**, size **10** in **White** (see Figure 17.11).

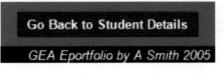

Figure 17.11: Adding a shape with a shadow

● You can adjust the position of the text by altering the size of the margins inside the shape. If your button is tall, you should increase the size of the margin above the text, forcing it down into the centre of the shape.

● Right-click the box and select **Format Autoshape**. Click on the **Text Box** tab and alter the **Top Internal Margin** until it looks correct.

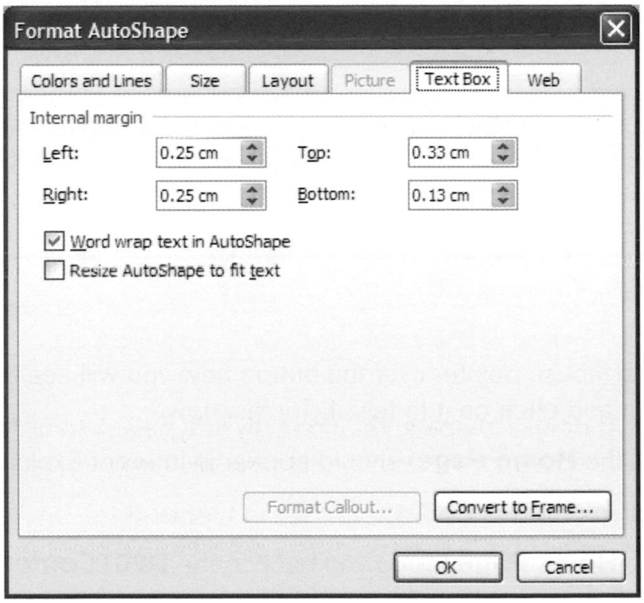

Figure 17.12: Adjusting AutoShape margins

Adding a hyperlink

The hyperlink is what will turn the ordinary red box into a button that does something. The box you have just created will link to the **Home Page (Index.html)** you have already created.

● Right-click the shape, making sure that no text cursor is displayed, and select **Hyperlink**.

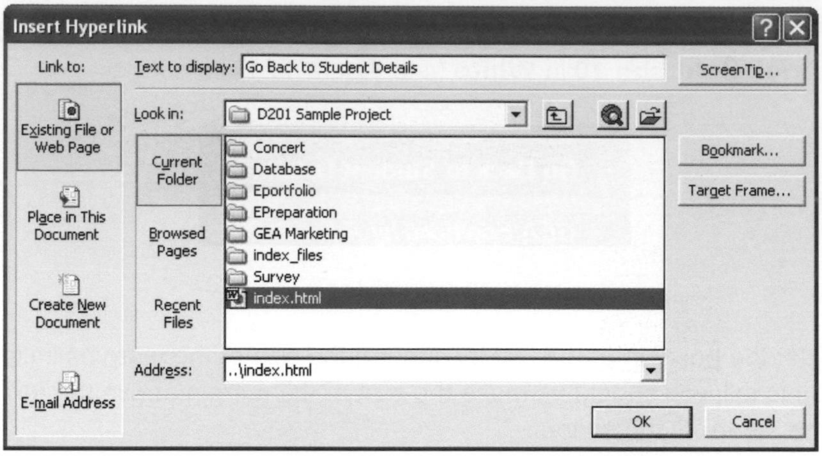

Figure 17.13: Inserting a hyperlink

▶ Select the **Index.html** file and click **OK**.

Important:

There are two types of address: **absolute** (the full path is given) and **relative** (the path is given in terms of the route from the current page, where **..** means 'go up a level'). You MUST save your files as .htm files, NOT .mht files, to ensure that all of your hyperlinks use relative addresses, otherwise the links may break when you upload the eportfolio!

▶ **Save** the file.

▶ When you hover the mouse pointer over the button now you will see a tip saying you can hold the **Ctrl** button and **click** on it to test it. Try this now.

The **Index.html** file (i.e. the **Home Page**) should appear in Internet Explorer.

▶ Close the Internet Explorer window.

▶ Add a button to the **Home Page** taking you back to the **D201Contents** page. Label it **Contents**. Format it in exactly the same way as the first button you created.

▶ Save the **Home Page** and test the new button.

Creating the Plan page

Now you need to create the first of your main pages: the **Plan** page.

▶ With the **Contents** page displayed in Word, click **File, Save as Web Page**. Make sure the **Save as type** is set to **Web Page**, and save the page under a new filename **D201Plan** in the **eportfolio** folder.

▶ Immediately change the title of the new page from **GEA Eportfolio Contents** to **Plan**.

▶ Save the file again. This will help prevent confusion between the two files.

Make the changes illustrated in Figure 17.14. You will need to split the left hand cell into 11 rows and merge the cells in the main area.

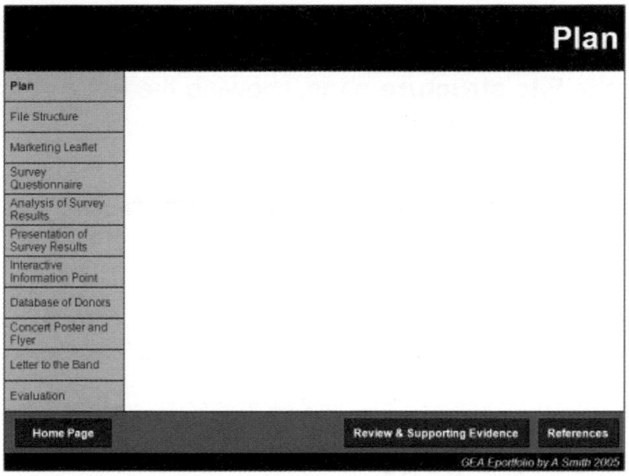

Figure 17.14: The project plan page

Removing a hyperlink

You need to remove the hyperlink at the bottom of this page and rename the button so that you can use it for something else.

 Right-click the edge of the button and select **Remove Hyperlink**.

 Rename it **References** and reduce the width to make it more suitable for the amount of text.

Copying objects using the Ctrl key

To create a new button you can use the **Ctrl** key to copy an object and the **Shift** key to move an object in a perfect vertical or horizontal direction.

 Hold down the **Ctrl** and **Shift** keys and drag the button over to the left. This will create an identical button and keep it exactly horizontally aligned with the original.

 Do the same thing again to create a third button on the far left, and rename them as shown in Figure 17.15.

Figure 17.15

Tip:

The **Home Page** link will take the user back to the **Contents** page rather than the **Student Details** page, as this is the page they will most likely need to return to.

Leave the page blank for now. You will come back to it later to insert a pdf of your plan when you have finished the project.

Creating the File Structure page

Now you need to create the **File structure** page, showing the folder structure that you created to hold the various elements in your eportfolio.

▶ Make sure that the **Plan** page is still selected.

▶ Click **File, Save As Web Page** and save the page (using the **Web Page** type) with the new filename **D201FileStructure** in **Eportfolio**.

▶ Immediately change the title of the new page from **Plan** to **File Structure**.

▶ Save the file again.

Adding a screenshot to a page

The Setup page will show how you have managed your files and folders when you first set up the project. You can use a screenshot of your file structure.

▶ Open Windows Explorer and take a screenshot of the folders you set up. Use the **Print Screen** key to copy the screen image to the clipboard.

▶ **Paste** the screenshot into the main cell of the web page.

▶ Place a brief description of the screenshot under the image.

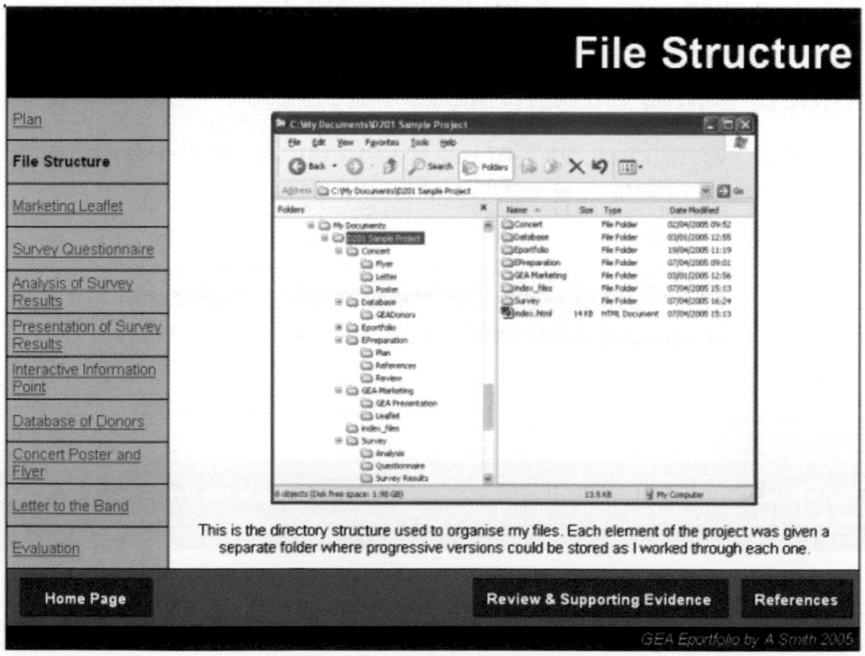

Figure 17.16

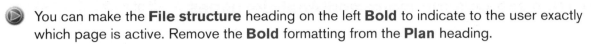

> You can make the **File structure** heading on the left **Bold** to indicate to the user exactly which page is active. Remove the **Bold** formatting from the **Plan** heading.

> Add a hyperlink to the **Home Page** button to link to the **D201Contents** file.

> **Save** the page.

Creating the GEA Leaflet page

> With the **D201FileStructure** page already open, save it again as **D201MarketingLeaflet** in the **Eportfolio** folder.

> Make the **Marketing Leaflet** heading on the left bold and remove the bold formatting from the **File Structure** heading.

Immediately change the title of the new file to **Marketing Leaflet** and save it again.

You need to include screenshots of both sides of the leaflet. Since one side fits well within the main section of the page, you could place another button at the bottom of the page linking it to a similar page showing the reverse side of the leaflet.

> Take a screenshot of the front page of the leaflet and paste it into the centre of the page.

> Add a button to access an image of the reverse side. Your finished page should look like Figure 17.17.

Figure 17.17: The D201MarketingLeaflet page

> Create an identical page and insert a screenshot of the reverse side of the leaflet. Remember to link the two pages together and to rename the button on the **Reverse** page.

> **Save** the **D201MarketingLeaflet** page and call the **Reverse** page **D201MarketingLeafletReverse**. Save this in the same folder.

Creating the Questionnaire and Analysis pages

▶ Create the **Survey Questionnaire** page in the same way, including a copy of the questionnaire in the main section of the page.

▶ Now create a new page for **D201SurveyAnalysis**. This will contain a link to the spreadsheet with the analysis of the questionnaire results. You should have already saved this spreadsheet as a web file in Chapter 16.

It would be nice to make the image of the pie chart behave as a hyperlink to the actual spreadsheet web file containing all of the details.

▶ Make your page look something like Figure 17.18.

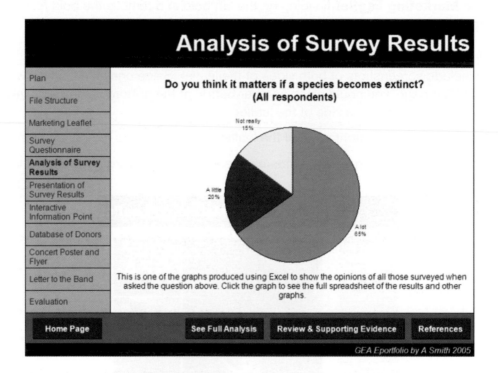

Figure 17.18: The Analysis page

Using an image as a hyperlink

You can add a hyperlink to the image, to provide an easy alternative way for the user to view the spreadsheet analysis file. You can put another link to the spreadsheet on the button labelled **See Full Analysis**. This helps it to be more user-friendly, catering for those who don't realise that the graph is a link too.

▶ Right-click the chart and select **Hyperlink**.

▶ Select the **SurveyAnalysis.htm** file that you saved in Chapter 16. You should find it in your **Eportfolio\Analysis** folder.

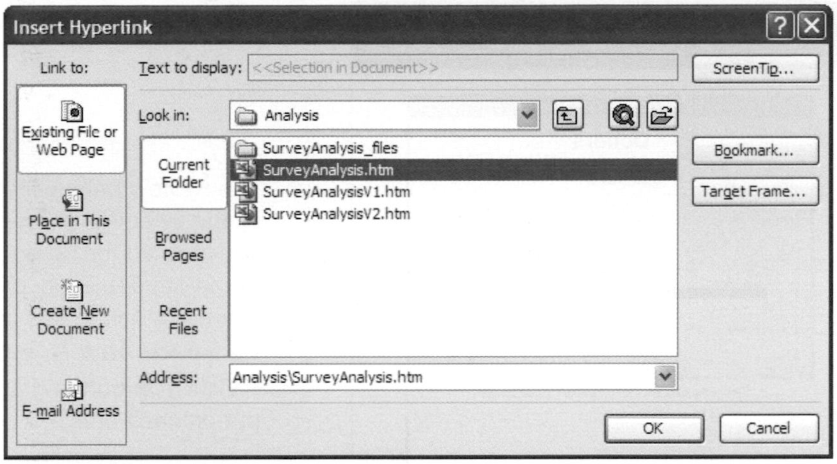

Figure 17.19: Creating a hyperlink from an image

▶ Click **OK**.

▶ Repeat the operation to create a hyperlink from the button as well.

The survey results and interactive presentations

▶ Complete the page for the survey results presentation in the same way by using a screenshot of the first slide as a hyperlink.

▶ Repeat the operation once more for the page with the interactive information point.

Creating the Database page

Since the database does not allow you to save everything as a web-compatible file, you need to take several screenshots of the table, input form, queries and reports in order to prove to the examiner that you did actually create it. You should explain what each screenshot shows.

The best way to do this is to create a page for the database with a link to another page containing all of the evidence behind it.

▶ Create the main database page similar to the one shown in Figure 17.20. A screenshot of one of the reports has been used to illustrate what this page is actually about. Try taking a screenshot of your own to insert on this page.

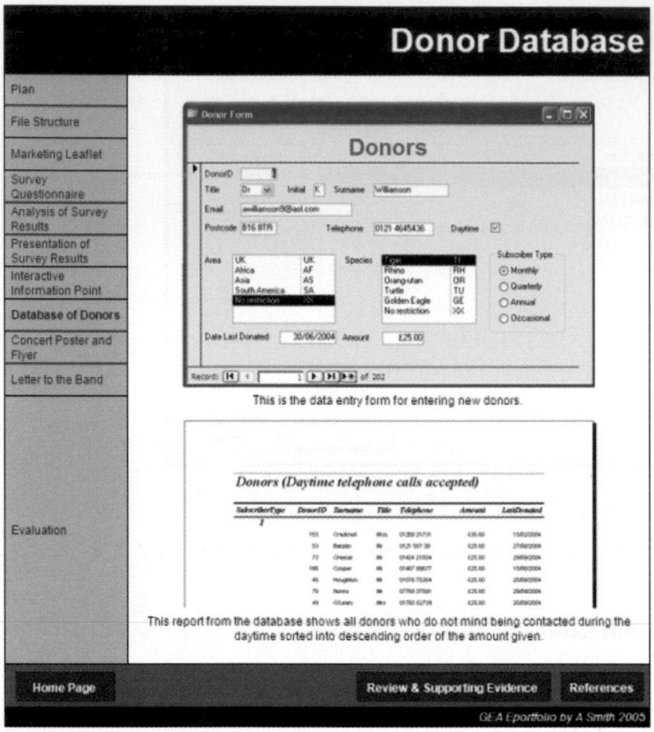

Figure 17.20: The Donor Database page

The Review page will contain all the evidence showing how you created the other elements of the project. Every page will eventually link to this new page via the **Review & Supporting Evidence** button that you have put on each one.

The new button called **Review & Supporting Evidence** will link to the page showing more of the database and its design.

Creating the Review page

- Create the page in the same way as before by saving the current page under a new filename, **D201Review**. Save it in the **Eportfolio** folder.
- Copy the format of the page shown in Figure 17.21.
- You need to include headings for each part of the project. It is here that you will later insert all the evidence that you have gathered throughout the project.

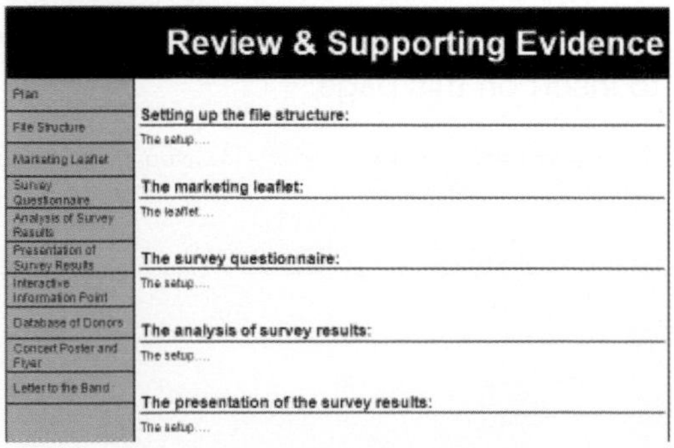

Figure 17.21: The review page

Inserting evidence of your database

Because the database cannot be run by the examiner, it is vital that you show screenshot evidence that you did actually create it and that it did what it was supposed to do. You can do this by taking screenshots of each of the database objects with a brief explanation where necessary:

- the table in **Design** view showing the data types and explaining any validation;
- your forms in **Form** view;
- your queries in **Design** view, showing the criteria you used to perform each query;
- your reports in **Report Preview**.

▷ Begin by opening the database and capturing an image of the table in **Design** view.

▷ Paste this into the **D201Review** page under the **Donor Database** heading.

▷ Write a simple explanation to go with it, highlighting the validation rules that you have used.

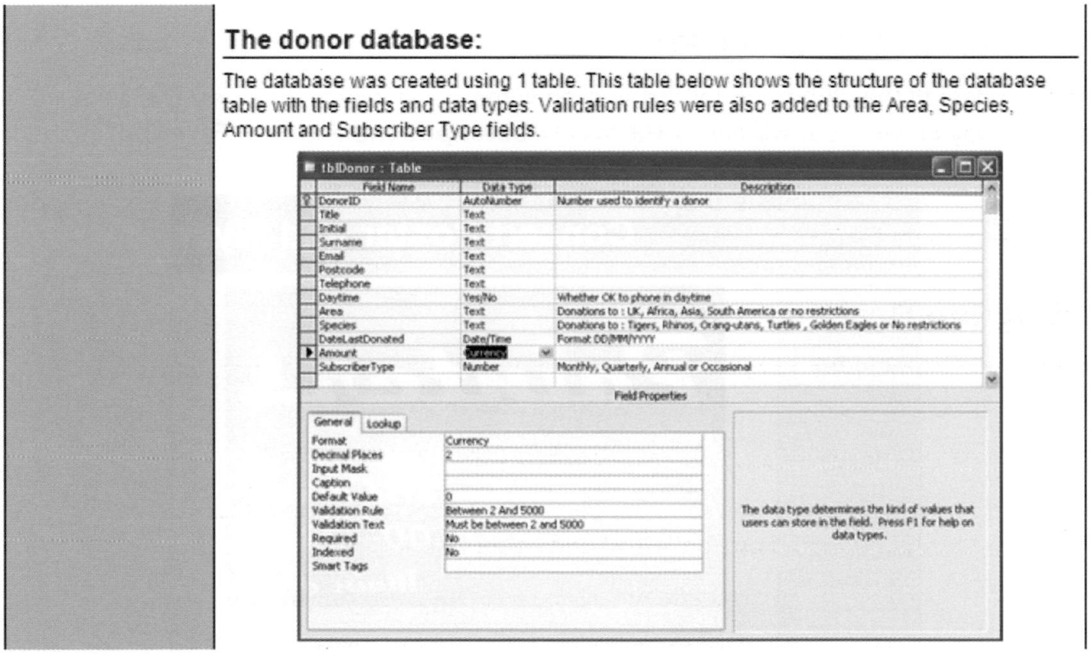

The donor database:

The database was created using 1 table. This table below shows the structure of the database table with the fields and data types. Validation rules were also added to the Area, Species, Amount and Subscriber Type fields.

Field Name	Data Type	Description
DonorID	AutoNumber	Number used to identify a donor
Title	Text	
Initial	Text	
Surname	Text	
Email	Text	
Postcode	Text	
Telephone	Text	
Daytime	Yes/No	Whether OK to phone in daytime
Area	Text	Donations to : UK, Africa, Asia, South America or no restrictions
Species	Text	Donations to : Tigers, Rhinos, Orang-utans, Turtles , Golden Eagles or No restrictions
DateLastDonated	Date/Time	Format DD/MM/YYYY
Amount	Currency	
SubscriberType	Number	Monthly, Quarterly, Annual or Occasional

Field Properties

General | Lookup

Format	Currency
Decimal Places	2
Input Mask	
Caption	
Default Value	0
Validation Rule	Between 2 And 5000
Validation Text	Must be between 2 and 5000
Required	No
Indexed	No
Smart Tags	

The data type determines the kind of values that users can store in the field. Press F1 for help on data types.

Figure 17.22: Adding evidence to support the development of your database

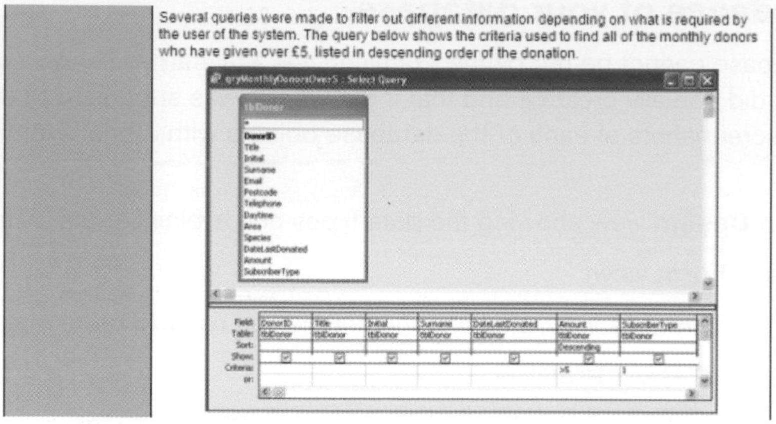

Figure 17.23: Evidence of one of the queries from the database

▶ Continue to add evidence until you have presented everything to the examiner.

▶ Save the file as **D201Review**.

The concert poster and flyer

You need to design the web page for this in exactly the same way as the rest. The links are made in the same way as well, but will link to **PaintersPoster.pdf** and **PaintersFlyer.pdf** respectively.

Figure 17.24: The concert poster page

▶ Once you have set up the links, try testing them using **Ctrl + Click**. You won't need to press the **Ctrl** button when you are viewing the pages in a browser such as Internet Explorer.

The letter to the band and evaluation pages

▷ Create the page for the letter by showing a screenshot of the letter in the main section of the page.

▷ Create the last page on the list of contents (**Evaluation**). You will put in the contents later.

Showing your sequence of development

You need to show evidence of how you built up each of the elements in the project. This is where you can use each of the different versions of the leaflet, presentations, spreadsheets and so on that you created as you went along.

You should put your development work in the **Review** page with the database evidence you added earlier.

As an example, this section will show you how to present the work for the leaflet. You should show your development work for everything.

Figure 17.25 shows the progression you took in making the final leaflet, with some explanation of any problems or mistakes and, most importantly, when and why you changed your mind as you went along. It is also a good idea to include scanned images of any sketches you made originally.

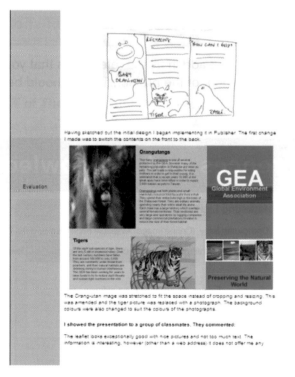

Figure 17.25: Showing your sequence of development

Each of the images used in the **D201Review** page for development are taken from the different versions you saved in Chapter 3 while you were making it.

Evaluation

Plan	**The eportfolio**
File Structure	**This is an evaluation of the final version of my eportfolio.**
Marketing Leaflet	**Outcomes**
Survey Questionnaire	I created the eportfolio in Word and checked it thoroughly using the following criteria:
Analysis of Survey Results	
Presentation of Survey Results	
Interactive Information Point	
Database of Donors	
Concert Poster and Flyer	
Letter to the Band	

Outcomes
I created the eportfolio in Word and checked it thoroughly using the following criteria:
- The whole portfolio has a consistent appearance
- The navigation buttons are in the same place on each page
- The layout is logical and easy to follow
- All the links work correctly
- Every page loads up quickly
- Most pages are short enough not to require excessive scrolling
- Spelling and grammar is correct

I referred to my plan while building the portfolio to ensure that all components were included.

Suggestions for improvement
It might have been better to have a separate link in the navigation bar for Evidence of development. The Evidence page could be bookmarked for each item.
Each page could have a 'Back' button taking the user back to the page previously visited. However, the user could use the existing button on the Internet Explorer toolbar.

Process
I underestimated the time it would take to do the questionnaire, analysis and presentations and I had to adjust my schedule. I also forgot to write down where I downloaded some of the images from and it took a long time to find them again.

Figure 18.3: The top of the Evaluation page

Good marks... ✓

You will get good marks if you:

- keep referring back to your plan and objectives to see if you met them;

- describe who each component is for, and consider whether it does its job;

- ask others for feedback and consider carefully whether you agree with it, and, if so, respond to it;

- make suggestions for how you could improve your project.

Bad marks... ✗

You will lose marks if you:

- do not refer to your plan;

- do not get feedback from others;

- do not show how you acted on the feedback, if it was appropriate.

Section Two
RESEARCHING INFORMATION

This unit is concerned with using ICT to

- plan,
- research,
- analyse, and
- present information

through work on a major project set by Edexcel.

In the next few chapters we will look at the different ways which you can use to research the information you need for a particular project.

Information sources

There are many ways of finding out information. For example you might use:

- ICT-based sources, such as the Internet, an intranet, CD-ROM or teletext;
- a paper-based source, such as a newspaper, magazine, brochure, encyclopaedia, directory or manual;
- a questionnaire that you have devised and handed out to people.

Discussion:

Where would you look up information on each of the following? Give a different answer for each one.

1. **Train times to Edinburgh**
2. **Arsenal's position in the Football League tables**
3. **What's on at the local cinema**
4. **The number of mountain gorillas living in the wild**
5. **A good deal on a laptop computer**
6. **Information on meteorites for a science project**
7. **The correct spelling of the word 'practice' (or is it 'practise'?) in the sentence "He is going to *practi–e* his saxophone for an hour tonight."**
8. **Holiday offers in Majorca**
9. **Ways to save money on the cost of heating a home**
10. **Where to find a particular book in the library**

Of course, you can find out almost all of these on the Internet. What an amazing source of information it is! But equally amazing is the fact that a large section of the population has never used the Internet and yet they still manage to conduct their daily lives quite happily, and find out all sorts of useful information.

Primary and secondary sources

Any research project involves gathering information for particular purposes, such as:

- to increase knowledge;
- to help with decision-making;
- to make recommendations.

You can use a wide range of information sources, both **primary** and **secondary**.

When you use information that has been produced by someone else, you are using a secondary source. Secondary sources include:

- paper-based sources such as newspapers, directories, books, maps;
- ICT-based sources such as the Internet, CDs or DVDs, databases;
- TV and radio.

You will have to select the most appropriate secondary sources, by asking questions such as:

- Is it unbiased?
- Is the information reliable and up-to-date?
- Can it be trusted?

Bias

Information is said to be **biased** if it is one-sided or expresses an opinion that does not reflect the entire situation or event that took place. A biased account of an event is unbalanced and will often be written to reflect the author's opinion, missing any information that may conflict with what they want you to believe or the message they want to get across.

For example, consider a football game between Ipswich Town and Norwich City where the score was 2-1 to Ipswich. After the match, two post-match reports are posted, one on each of the official websites. It is likely that the Norwich report would be written by a team fan, who may claim that the match was very much theirs and it was just an unlucky result. The Ipswich fan, on the other hand, may write that it was an absolute trouncing and that Norwich were lucky to get even one goal!

It would be sensible then, if researching this game, to dismiss both reports as biased.

Question:

Why would the Norwich fan want to write an unbalanced report of the game? (Hint: think of their audience.)

Reliability

Always check when the information you have found was written. Is it still accurate? Some information dates very quickly, but other information may never date. For example, if you were researching a company and found information that its share prices rocketed six months ago, that is not a reliable indicator of how the company is doing today. Someone's personal diary, however, will never date, even if they lived one hundred or more years ago.

Trustworthiness

You need to ask yourself whether the source of your information can be trusted. It may be that it comes from an organisation or individual who has a very rose-tinted view of what is really going on. For example, would you book a holiday in a Spanish beach resort from a brochure you had never heard of? You may read that it has a wonderful view of the sea and that it is close to all amenities. Several people have booked such holidays to find that there is only a glimpse of the sea over the run-down high-rise hotels outside their window. They have also been sent to hotels miles from anywhere and 10 minutes from the beach in a fast car!

Saving and using information

You may use paper-based sources to find information for a project. You can look up information in a book or encyclopaedia, or you might need to find information that has to be up-to-date, such as travel timetables or this year's holiday destination special offers.

To take the information home, you could use any of the following methods:

- Borrow the book, if it is available for loan. The advantage of this is that you will be able to browse through it at your leisure and use the passages that you need at a time that is convenient for you.

- Photocopy the pages containing relevant information. This has the advantage that you don't have to carry several heavy books home. Also, if the book is a reference book like an encyclopaedia you will not be allowed to take it out of the library. The disadvantage is that you may have to pay for the use of the photocopier, and it may be in use or out of order.

- Make your own notes while you are in the library. You can make notes from several different books or pages. The disadvantage of this is that you may find, when you get home, that you wish you had made notes on more of the information, or you may need to go back to the library again to check that you have copied the information accurately.

- If a scanner is available, scan the pages that you need (using OCR software to convert the scanned picture to text), and save the file on a floppy disk. Later, you can edit the information as required.

Practical work:

Go to the library and look at how several different newspapers cover the same story. Make notes on the differences. Do you think any of the accounts are biased? Are some of them written with a particular readership in mind?

Many of the paper-based sources that you will use to find information are available in your school library or the local public library. If you have not visited either, this week would be a good time to try them out.

You will find both ICT- and paper-based sources of information in the library. Paper-based sources include:

- reference books;
- dictionaries;
- encyclopaedias;
- directories;
- newspapers;
- magazines;
- newsletters;
- instruction manuals;
- card indexes.

You will probably be able to find all of these in the library, except the last – if your library is up-to-date they will have switched from a card-based catalogue to a computer-based one.

ICT-based sources include CD-ROMs and, of course, the Internet.

Card-based catalogue

A card-based catalogue typically contains a card for each book in the library, giving the title, author, subject matter or category (e.g. Fiction, Technology) and, if it is a non-fiction work, its Dewey decimal code. There may be three separate card index catalogues, sequenced by title, author and subject.

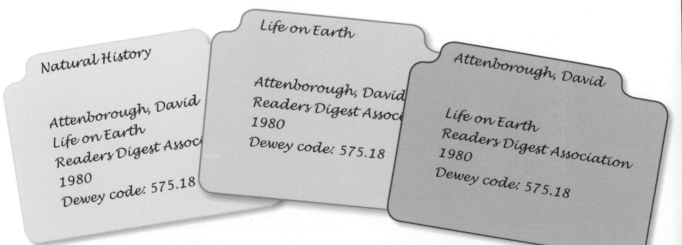

The Dewey decimal system

Most public, school and college libraries use a system of arranging non-fiction books invented by Melvil Dewey, an American librarian, in 1876. The system is referred to as The **Dewey Decimal Classification Scheme**. In the Dewey system, all books on the same subject are found in the same place, and books on similar subjects are found nearby.

A three-digit number is given to each subject; this can be made longer by adding a decimal point followed by more numbers – the longer the number after the decimal point, the more detailed the subject.

First of all, knowledge is divided up into ten main sections as follows:

Section Number	Subjects included
000	General: encyclopaedias, directories, books of facts and records, computers
100	Philosophy and psychology: books about ideas, thinking and the mind
200	Religion: religions and beliefs
300	Social issues: books about how society works and functions
400	Languages
500	Science: maths, astronomy, physics, chemistry, nature, plants, birds, animals, the weather
600	Technology: machines and inventions, electronics, medicine and the human body, farming, pets, food and cookery
700	The Arts: drawing, painting, photography, music, dance, theatre, hobbies, sport
800	Literature: poems, plays and critical works
900	History and countries: including explorers and biographies

Each of these is then divided into ten, as in the following example for Science:

Section Number	Subjects included
500	Natural science & mathematics
510	Mathematics
520	Astronomy & allied sciences
530	Physics
540	Chemistry & allied sciences
550	Earth sciences
560	Palcontology & paleozoology
570	Life sciences
580	Botanical sciences
590	Zoological sciences

Each of these more general divisions is then divided up again, to allow for easier location of more specific topics, for example:

Section Number	Subjects included
570	Life sciences
571	Not assigned or no longer used
572	Human races
573	Physical anthropology
574	Biology
575	Evolution & genetics
576	Microbiology
577	General nature of life
578	Microscopy in biology
579	Collection and preservation

These subjects can then become even more specific by adding a decimal point and more numbers, for example:

Section Number	Subjects included
574.1	Physiology
574.2	Pathology

The more numbers after the decimal point, the more specific the subject. Fortunately you do not have to remember all these numbers. All libraries have subject indexes, which are generally alphabetical lists of subjects with their numbers.

Figure 20.1: Library books classified under the Dewey decimal system

Computer-based catalogue

Most County Library services offer computer-based catalogues that can be accessed within the libraries or from your own PC. This means that you can search for books, view your own library account and renew your books from home.

A computer-based catalogue is basically a database – that is, a collection of information structured into fields and records, and stored on a computer. The database software enables you to search the data using criteria to find what you are looking for.

For example, Suffolk County Council provides an on-line library service called LibCat. When you reach the web site you can choose from a variety of services.

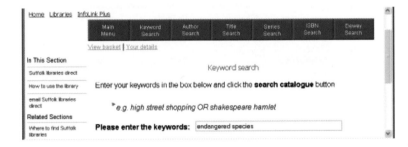

Figure 20.2: Searching a computer-based catalogue

If you want to find all books written by a particular author, you click the **Author Search** button and then type in the name of the author:

Figure 20.3: Searching for an author

The books by this author, and the availability of each book, will be displayed:

Suffolk libraries direct	Title Information				
How to use the library					
email Suffolk libraries direct	**Author**	Attenborough, David			
Related Sections	**Title**	Life on earth, a natural history			
Where to find Suffolk libraries	**Dewey Class Number**	575			
Suffolk Infolink Plus	**Publication**	Collins, 1990			
Cyberlibrary	**ISBN**	0002190915			
Contact Us	**Category**	SCI:Bio			
Visitors Book	**Physical Description**	319p, ill, 26cm			
Site Tools	**Format:**	Hardback			
Search	**Subject**	Evolution			

	Copy Availability				
Library	**Shelf Location**	**Status**	**Duedate**	**Category**	
Ipswich County Library	575	On Shelf		Adult Non Fiction	
Lowestoft Central Library	Science	On Shelf		Adult Non Fiction	
Mildenhall Library		On Shelf		Adult Non Fiction	

Figure 20.4: Book availability

Newspapers and magazines

Newspapers are an ideal source for the latest updates on news items. They employ journalists who specialise in certain areas, and often include one-off features about a particular topic. You can also look out for special supplements that the broadsheet newspapers publish regularly – for example, the *Guardian* has a Media section on Mondays and an Online section on Thursdays.

Public, school and college libraries usually stock back copies of the more popular broadsheet newspapers. These cannot normally be taken out on loan but can be used for reference whilst you are in the library.

Several of the newspapers now have on-line versions available on the World Wide Web, for example:

- **www.guardian.co.uk**
- **www.telegraph.co.uk**
- **www.timesonline.co.uk**
- **www.independent.co.uk**
- **www.observer.co.uk**

Back copies of several newspapers, for example the *Guardian* and *The Sunday Times*, are also available on CD-ROM.

Specialist magazines often have in-depth articles about particular topics. Most libraries keep back copies of a selection of titles which can be used for reference.

Discussion:

What are the advantages and disadvantages of an online newspaper compared with a printed one?

Figure 20.5: Guardian *online*

Practical work:

Go to the library and look up some information on environmental organisations such as the WWF, Greenpeace and Friends of the Earth.

What are their objectives?

What methods are they using to achieve their objectives?

What action are they taking?

The Internet consists of a huge number of computers connected together all over the world. You can connect to the Internet only at certain points, via a phone or cable service provider.

The best-known part of the Internet is the World Wide Web. This consists of hundreds of millions of web pages stored on computers all over the world, which you can access from your own computer. Virtually all large companies and organisations have websites, as do many small companies and private individuals.

Hardware and software for Internet access

To access the Internet you will need some hardware:

- A computer connected to a phone line.

- A modem, which translates the digital signals from your computer to an analogue signal transmitted over the phone line. Another modem at the other end translates the signal back from analogue to digital.

- Alternatively, you may use an ISDN or broadband line. You can also connect to the Internet using a WAP phone or TV and set-top box.

You will need some software:

- A browser, such as Internet Explorer.

- E-mail software, such as Microsoft Outlook, if you want to send emails

Using a web address

If you know the website address, the easiest way to get there is to type it into the **address box**.

Figure 21.1: Typing a web address

 **Tip:**

To go to an address in the format **www.*name*.com**, just type *name*, hold down **Ctrl** and press **Enter**. The rest is put in for you!

Every web page has a unique address, known as the **URL** – for **Uniform Resource Locator**. This has distinct parts separated by dots, each part having a special significance. A typical address is:

http://www.bbc.co.uk

The first part is the protocol used by the Internet for sending and receiving data between computers. The most common protocol is **http://**, which stands for **Hypertext Transfer Protocol**. There's no need to type in **http://** as the browser adds it automatically. Some addresses may have **https://** for a secure page with sensitive information, or **ftp://** for file transfer.

www means World Wide Web and is in most but not all web page addresses.

bbc.co.uk is the domain name showing the organisation owning the site and has several parts:

- **co** is the type of site, in this case a commercial organisation. International company domain names generally end in **.com**.

- Some other codes are **gov** for government, **org** for non-profit organisations, **ac** for educational sites (**edu** in the USA), or **sch** for schools.

- If the site is neither **.com** nor US-based there is usually a country code: **uk** for the UK, **fr** for France, **de** for Germany, **es** for Spain, **ch** for Switzerland, **ie** for Ireland, and so on.

> **Tip:**
>
> New codes you may see are **biz**, **plc**, **info**, **tv** and **me**.
>
> You will have heard of **dotcom** companies – this is often misspelt **dot.com** which would have to be pronounced **dot dot com**.

There may also be the name of a file on the end of the address, such as **/index.htm**. Web pages are written in a language called **HTML** (for **Hypertext Markup Language**) and each page is a file usually ending in **.htm**.

Here are some sample URLs – you can probably guess whom they belong to.

http://www.bbc.co.uk

http://www.worldwildlife.org

http://www.cam.ac.uk

http://www.payne-gallway.co.uk

ftp://ftp.hq.nasa.gov

http://www.museum-london.org.uk

http://www.harvard.edu

http://www.louvre.fr

Using hyperlinks

Most web pages have hyperlinks, which enable you to jump to another page, or back to the top of the same page if it's quite long. When you move the mouse pointer around the screen, the shape changes from an arrow to a hand when it is over a 'hot' area. These are usually text underlined in blue, but may also be pictures. When you click on a hot area, the browser jumps to that page.

Try logging on to the WWF-UK home page (www.wwf-uk.org) and moving the pointer over the page – there are dozens of hyperlinks!

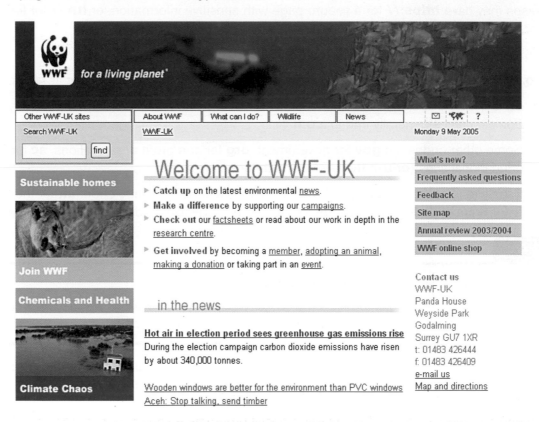

Figure 21.2: The WWF Home page

Using a search engine

A search engine is software that allows you to type a word or phrase into a box and then view all the results that it finds.

Notice that the WWF Home page shown in Figure 21.2 has its own search engine – you can type in a word or phrase to search the site.

 Try typing **endangered species** into the box to look for stories about this subject.

My goodness! This could be your first taste of information overload: over 150 stories.

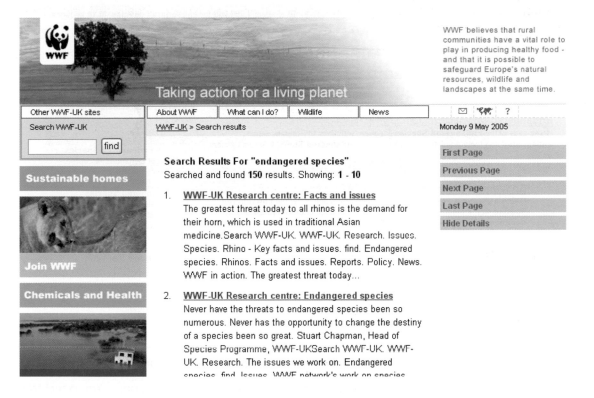

Figure 21.3: Searching the WWF website

Google

One of the best known and most powerful search engines is Google.

Search engines keep an index of keywords. Special programs – known as **crawlers**, **spiders** or **bots** – continually run all over the Web collecting keywords from each website. These embedded keywords (called **meta tags**), invisible in normal view, are put on the site by the designer so as to be found by crawlers and cause the site to pop up on search results pages as often as possible. With vague or misleading keywords a page will often appear unexpectedly.

Enter the address **www.google.co.uk**

Try the same search – enter **endangered species** into the **Search** box.

Google finds over 4 million references. Now that IS information overload! However, the first few results direct you to some key sites.

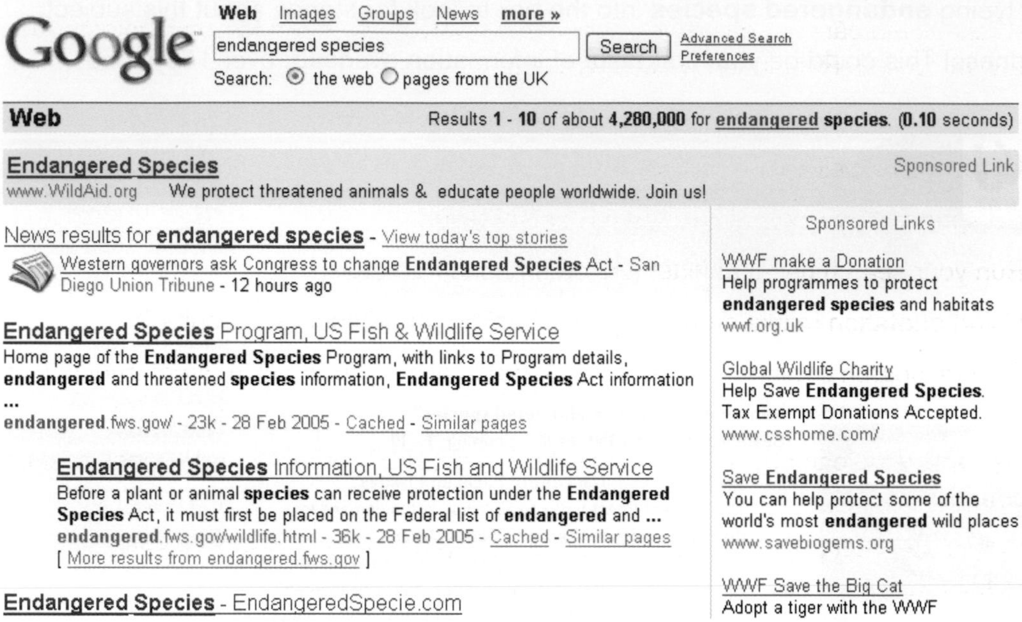

Figure 21.4: Using Google

Refining a search

Suppose you wanted to find out about jaguars in the jungles of Central and South America.

You could try just typing in **jaguar**, but this will find mostly sites to do with cars. You need to cut down the number of results that are not relevant.

▶ Try typing **jaguar +cat –car**

This finds all the sites that include the words **jaguar** and **cat** but do NOT include the word **car**.

An alternative is to use the Google Advanced Search.

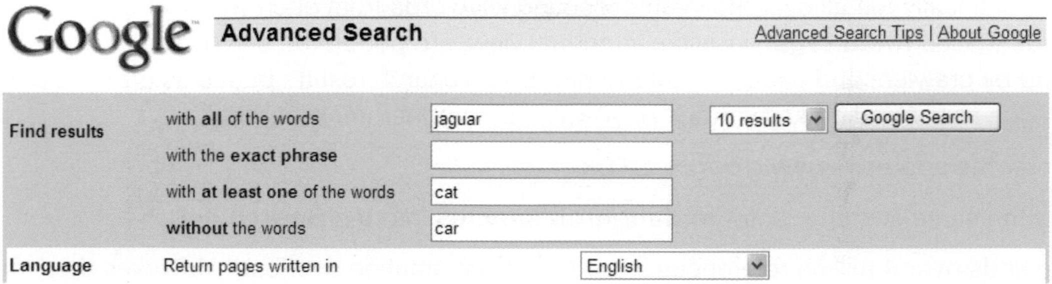

Figure 21.5: The Google Advanced Search

Tips for searching

You must take some care in setting up your search query – you need to communicate exactly what you want to find. Remember these useful tips:

- If possible do not use connecting words like **the** and **an**.
- Check your spelling.
- Be specific. Try a few different word combinations.
- Run your search using at least two different search tools.
- Using quotation marks around a phrase will get more accurate results.
- Several search engines (e.g. **www.ask.com**) allow you to ask a direct question and then search for the results.
- Try using Boolean operators such as **AND**, **OR**, **NOT**, or the **+** and **–** signs to refine your search.
- Remember that after an initial search you may have to make a further search within those results.

Saving your results

You will often need to save or print the results of your research to refer to later. You can select the text on a web page, then right-click and select **Copy**. Then paste the text into your own word-processed document. Make a note of the address where you copied it from so that you can acknowledge the source of your information.

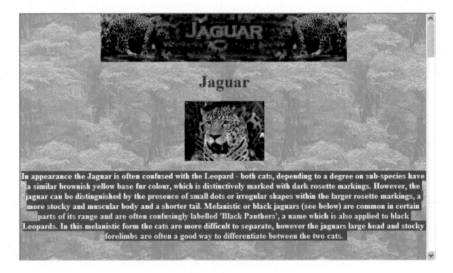

Figure 21.6: Selecting text on a web page

Saving a web page

Internet Explorer will allow you to save any web page to the hard drive of your computer or to a floppy disk. The saved page is just like any other document so you can open the browser and view the page while you are working offline.

 Open the page in Internet Explorer and choose **Save As** from the **File** menu.

 The **Save Web Page** dialogue box appears as shown below.

Save Web Page	? X
Save in: 🗀 endangered species ▾	◐ 🗂 🗁 ▥▾

My Recent Documents
Desktop
My Documents
My Computer
My Network

File name:	species ▾	Save
Save as type:	Web Page, complete (*.htm;*.html) ▾	Cancel
Encoding:	Western European (Windows) ▾	

Figure 21.7: Saving a web page

 Navigate to the folder in which you want to store your saved documents. Enter a filename.

 Make sure that **Web Page, complete** appears in the **Save as type** box. Click **Save**. You have saved the whole web page, including any pictures.

To view the saved web page:

 Open Internet Explorer.

 From the **File** menu, select **Work Offline**. From the same menu select **Open**.

> **Tip:**
>
> If you are working offline, Internet Explorer will not try to connect to the Internet. You should change this setting back when you have finished browsing your files.

 Click the **Browse** button to navigate to the folder where you saved the web page and related graphics. Select the file with the Internet Explorer symbol and click **Open**.

 Click **OK** on the **Open** dialogue box.

Sometimes you may just want to save a picture from a website.

- ▶ Right-click the image and choose **Save Picture As**.
- ▶ Find the folder in which you want to save the picture and click **Save**.

Storing the URL

Sometimes you may want to store the URL (address) of a particular web page so that you can return to it quickly at any time. In Netscape Navigator, this is called saving a **bookmark**. In Internet Explorer, you add the page to a list of **Favorites**.

You can practise adding a page to the **Favorites** list, and then using the saved link.

- ▶ Load Internet Explorer.
- ▶ Click the **Favorites** button on the toolbar. (If you haven't got one, you can press **Ctrl+I** instead.)

Figure 21.8

The **Favorites** pane will open on the left-hand side of the screen.

Now suppose you have found a page that you want to save.

- ▶ Click the **Add** button (see Figure 21.9) or select **Favorites**, **Add to Favorites** from the menu.

Figure 21.9

221

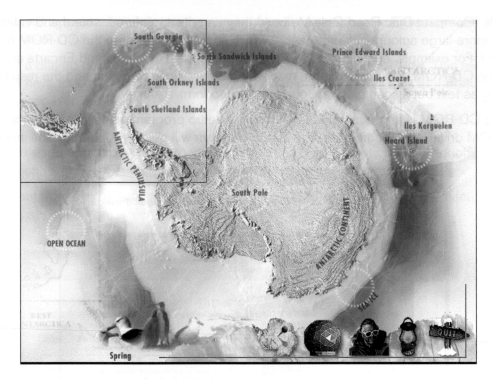

Fig 22.2: A CD-ROM about the Antarctic

Here, for each of the four seasons, you can view a panorama of a zone and click in circled zones to find out more about the wildlife there.

Figure 22.3: Life around the sea ice

Using information from a CD-ROM

If you want to use one of the pictures for your own work, you have various options:

 Take a screenshot using the **Prt Src** button or screen-capture software.

 Try right-clicking the picture you want. This often gives you the option to save the picture. You can save this on a floppy disk or a suitable folder and later insert it into a document. To do this, you would select **Insert**, **Picture**, **From File** on Word's menu bar, and then select the file you saved.

You can save text in the same way; this will probably be saved as a **txt** file, which you can edit. You should not paste text from another source straight into your final document – use it to make your own notes.

Using a CD-ROM encyclopaedia

An encyclopaedia on CD-ROM is a fast and convenient way to look up information of all sorts in the form of text, graphics and multimedia. A well-known encyclopedia is Microsoft's Encarta. This installs itself with the option of running it from CD to save on hard disk space.

Choosing a topic in the list or entering it in the **Find** box shows the main article on that subject. Links take you to related topics and allow you to play sound files. Clicking **Multimedia** on the toolbar gives a choice of animations that explain different topics.

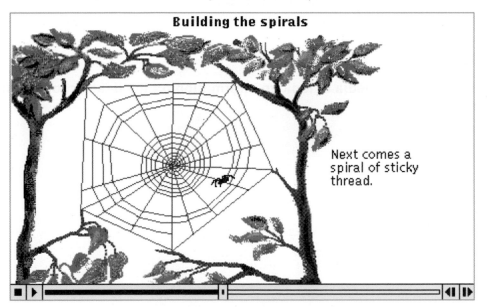

Figure 22.4: Playing an Encarta animation

225

Copyright

Normally it is quite all right to use text and images that you have copied from a book, CD or the Internet for your own work, so long as you do not intend to publish it or make a profit out of it. You should, however, always give the source of your material.

Look back to Chapter 17 to see how you can set out a bibliography detailing your sources of information and graphics.

You must respect the author's copyright. If you intend to publish work containing text or images produced by someone else, you should ask for their permission. You may have to pay a fee.

CD-ROM v. Internet

When you use a CD-ROM for information to use in your own work, you need to ask yourself:

- Is the information up-to-date?
- Is it accurate?

The information may not be as up-to-date as that downloaded from the Internet. If you are looking up a phone number on a directory CD-ROM this may be important, but if you are looking up facts about 1000-year-old castles, it may not be. Information on a CD-ROM published by a reputable company is likely to have been checked thoroughly and be accurate. In contrast, there is very little control over who puts what on the Internet and some of the information may be completely wrong, biased or out-of-date. You may need to check its accuracy by looking at other websites.

Practical task:

Use a CD-ROM encyclopaedia to look up information on the destruction of forests and what this leads to.

Chapter 23 – Accuracy

You must make sure that the information you include in any document is accurate. This means:

- You must check that the *content* is correct – for example the correct figures must be given in a presentation or a report, and the correct directions to a site given in a business letter. This may involve some investigation and research, perhaps consulting other people.

- You must check the *accuracy of typing*. Your document must be typed in without any spelling, punctuation, grammar or formatting errors. There are software tools, such as spelling and grammar checkers, that can help with this.

It is important not to send out documents that have spelling mistakes in them. Prospective employers, for example, will not be impressed by a CV containing errors of spelling, punctuation or grammar. A company that sends out documents with mistakes in them will make a bad impression on customers.

Automatic spelling and grammar checking

When you type a document using a word processor such as Word, misspelt words will be underlined with a wavy red line, and grammar errors with a green wavy line. However, a word processor cannot find every misspelt word, and sometimes it thinks words are misspelt even when they are not.

Exercise:

Read each of these sentences. Find all the mistakes of spelling, punctuation or grammar. (You should find at least 16!) Which of the mistakes will NOT be found by a spelling or grammar checker? Why not?

a.   It is easy to to make miss steaks in yore document.

b.   Last Monday I wnet to Manchster last MOnday to do some shop .

c.   Dont forget to pick up Johns' trumpet on the way home.He needs for Band Practise this evening..

d.   they're giving away ten mobbile phone's at the Suffulk Show Thursday.

e.   Their going to   take there overnigt bags and stay over at Chris's House.

Limitations of spelling and grammar checkers

The spelling checker in a word processor checks the spelling of each word by comparing it with words held in its dictionary. You may come across some of these problems:

- It may not recognise words spelt the English way, like 'colour' instead of 'color'.

- It may not recognise some proper names like Jumal or Sproughton, and so will underline them even if they are correct.

- It does not pick up words that are in the dictionary but are wrong in the context you have written them. For example, **shop** instead of **shopping** in sentence (b) in the previous exercise.

- It may not pick up all punctuation errors; for example **Johns'** instead of **John's** in sentence (c).

- It may not pick up extra spaces between words.

- It may not pick up missing words or repeated words.

> **Note:**
>
> If the spelling checker does not recognise a proper name that you frequently use, you can **add it to the dictionary**. You may not be able to add words to the dictionary if you are working on a school network.

Here are the corrected sentences.

a. It is easy to make mistakes in your document.

b. I went to Manchester last Monday to do some shopping.

c. Don't forget to pick up John's trumpet on the way home. He needs it for Band Practice this evening.

d. They're giving away ten mobile phones at the Suffolk Show on Thursday.

e. They're going to take their overnight bags and stay over at Chris's house.

Print Preview

Before printing a document you also need to check its layout. You must remember that what you see on the screen is not the whole piece of paper. To see how your documents will look you need to use the **Print Preview** feature.

Print Preview

◉ Open your letter to The Painters and click the **Print Preview** button on the **Standard** toolbar.

Your document appears as an image of a piece of A4 paper.

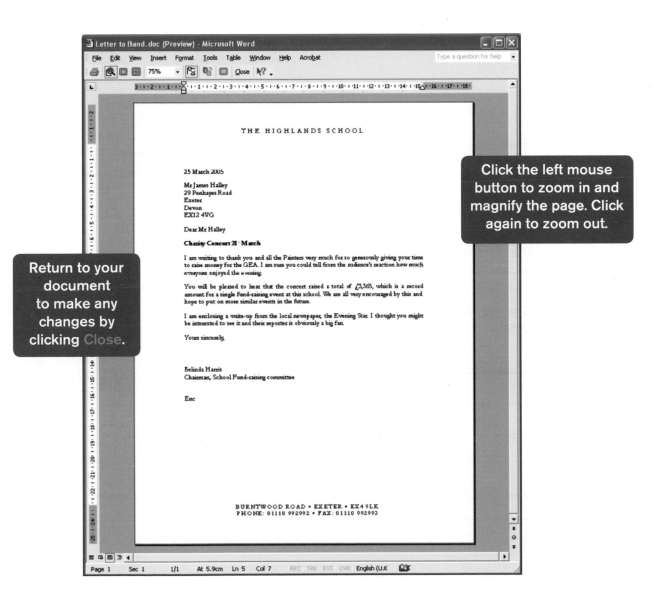

Return to your document to make any changes by clicking Close.

Click the left mouse button to zoom in and magnify the page. Click again to zoom out.

Figure 23.1

Proofreading

The software tools that you have been using to check your documents will not guarantee that there are no errors. To check that your document makes sense, that it is correctly laid out and meets your purpose, you must also proofread it carefully. As a proofreader, you mark the document by hand to indicate the changes that are needed. There is a British Standard for proofreaders' symbols; the most commonly used ones are reproduced in Figure 23.2.

Correction	Textual Mark	Margin Mark
Deletion	 / through character *or* ⊢⊣ through words to be deleted	 ⌒
Start new paragraph	 ⌐	 ⌐
Insertion	 ⋏	 ⋏
Run on (no new paragraph)	 ⌒	 ⌒
Change to capital letters	 ≡	 ≡
Change to lower case	encircle characters to be changed	 ≢
Indent	 ⊏	 ⊏
Use italic letters	 ____ under characters	 ⌣⌣
Use bold letters	 ∿∿∿∿∿ under characters	 ∿∿
Centre text	 [Enclosing matter to be centred] 	[ ]

Figure 23.2: Proof correction marks

You should get into the habit of using these as they are a clear, quick way of reminding yourself of corrections that need to be made. You really need a pencil with a very fine point to make the marks in exactly the right place.

It is often a good idea to ask someone else to check your work for you – we often see what we want to see, not what is really there!

- A good proofreader should check for obvious mistakes, such as spelling, grammar and typographical errors, and also for clarity, sense and consistency.

- For example, a section of a report may refer to a diagram or a chart that has actually been taken out at some stage. It is easy to lose track and not remove the reference.

- Another potential area for mistakes is the use of the wrong word. In Microsoft Word Help you can view a list of commonly confused words, for example 'practice' and 'practise' are often confused, as are 'affect' and 'effect'.

- Look out for formatting errors such as the wrong size or type of font, wrong use of italic or bold text, extra blank lines between paragraphs and so on.

Final checks

After correcting a document, and before you print it for the final time, remember to:

- proofread it again;
- look at it on screen in **Print Preview** mode to make sure the page layout looks correct;
- save it;
- make sure you have the correct stationery loaded in the printer.

Exercise:

Here is a first attempt at the letter to the band.

(a) (i) Proofread this letter. Mark the corrections on a photocopy of the letter.

25 March 14, 2005

Mr James Halley
29 Penhayes Road
Exeter
Devon
EX12 4VG

Dear Mrr Halley

Charity Concert 21st March

I am writing to thank you and all the Panters very much for so generously giving you're time to erase money for the GEA. I am sure you could tell from the audiences reaction how much every one enjoyed the evening. You will be pleased to hear that the concert raised a total of of £3,365, which is a record amount for a single fund-raising event at this school. We are all very encouraged by this and hope to put on more similar events in the future..

I am enclosing a write-up from the local newspaper. I thought you might be interested see it and their reporter is obviously a big fan!!

    Yours sincerly,

Belinda Harris

Chairman, School Fund-raising committee

(ii) Write down one error that a grammar checker will find.

(iii) Write down one spelling error that the spell checker will not find.

(b) A colleague suggests that you make some more changes.

(i) The first paragraph is too long.

Decide a sensible place for a new paragraph to start.

Use ⌐ to indicate this.

The name of the newspaper, the 'Evening Star' should be inserted after the word 'newspaper'. Show this on the letter.

Index

Index